T0291515

Systemic Risk

History, Measurement and Regulation

Systemic Risk

History, Measurement and Regulation

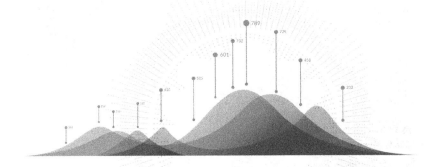

Yvonne Kreis
Schüllermann and Partner, Germany

Dietmar Leisen
Johannes Gutenberg University of Mainz, Germany

Jorge Ponce
Central Bank of Uruguay, Uruguay

 **World Scientific**

NEW JERSEY · LONDON · SINGAPORE · BEIJING · SHANGHAI · HONG KONG · TAIPEI · CHENNAI · TOKYO

Published by

World Scientific Publishing Co. Pte. Ltd.

5 Toh Tuck Link, Singapore 596224

USA office: 27 Warren Street, Suite 401-402, Hackensack, NJ 07601

UK office: 57 Shelton Street, Covent Garden, London WC2H 9HE

British Library Cataloguing-in-Publication Data
A catalogue record for this book is available from the British Library.

SYSTEMIC RISK
History, Measurement and Regulation

ISBN 978-981-120-105-9

For any available supplementary material, please visit
https://www.worldscientific.com/worldscibooks/10.1142/11301#t=suppl

Desk Editor: Shreya Gopi

Typeset by Stallion Press
Email: enquiries@stallionpress.com

Dedicated to

P. B. I.

Maike and Kayla

Maite

Acknowledgements

The authors thank Fabiana Gómez, Peter Raupach and the Research Department at the Superintendency of Banks and Financial Institutions Chile for comments on earlier versions of this book. They are particularly grateful to Simon Rother for his careful reading and suggestions that significantly improved the book. Finally, we appreciate the language editing services by Linda Pesante.

Contents

List of Figures

List of Tables

About the Authors

Yvonne Kreis currently is a Senior Consultant with Schüllermann & Partners in Mainz, Germany. Prior to this, she was a post-doctoral researcher (Habilitandin) at Gutenberg University in Mainz, Germany. She received her Ph.D. in economics from Gutenberg University for a thesis on the forecast quality of financial analysts. Her research focuses on systemic risk, financial crises, and portfolio strategy. She has also conducted several (international) research projects on the influence of trust and distrust in finance. Her research has been published in the *Journal of Financial Stability* among others.

Dietmar Leisen currently is Professor of Banking at Gutenberg University in Mainz, Germany. Prior to this, he was an Assistant Professor of Finance in the Faculty of Management at McGill University in Montreal, Canada during 2000–2004 and a Postdoctoral Fellow at Stanford University's Hoover Institution during 1998–2000. He received a Ph.D. in economics from the University of Bonn, Germany in 1998. His research interests include quantitative finance, financial stability, and corporate governance. His research articles have been published in many international journals, including the *Journal of Financial Stability*, *Quantitative Finance*, the *Journal of Economic Dynamics and Control*, and the *Journal of Economic Theory*.

Jorge Ponce currently is Head of the Financial Stability Department (since 2012) and Head of the Research Department (since 2019) at the Central Bank of Uruguay. Before 2012 he served as economist at the Central Bank. Jorge is also affiliated with the University of the Republic of Uruguay as Professor of Economics and Finance, and with the National Agency for

Systemic Risk: History, Measurement and Regulation

Research and Innovation in Uruguay. He received a Ph.D. in Economics from the Toulouse School of Economics in 2009. His research has been published in the *Journal of Financial Intermediation*, the *Journal of Financial Stability*, the *Journal of Banking and Finance*, and the *Journal of Financial Services Research*, among others.

Introduction

Financial instability has direct and severe consequences for financial systems. Historically, such episodes of instability are most worrisome when they spread to the real economy and affect the real sector. Data from previous systemic crises shows high costs to society in terms of lost production, fiscal deficits, inflation, and the time needed for an economic recovery. Moreover, financial crises also affect public health: Empirical evidence shows that suicide and heart attack rates are higher after financial instability events, and that these events seem to have a long-lasting impact on society.

The severity of its consequences creates strong interest in understanding financial instability in mitigating risk and in minimizing the negative consequences of systemic risk. However, episodes of financial instability occur infrequently, impeding statistical analysis. Moreover, such episodes appear to come in many different forms. First, financial instability has occurred historically both in developed and in developing countries. More broadly, it has appeared in different types of financial systems, both market-based (e.g., the U.S.) and banking-based systems (e.g., Europe, Latin America). It has occurred at different times in the past and is still an important topic now. It spreads through different propagation, contagion, and amplification mechanisms. Finally, it has occurred at different stages of economic, financial, and technological development.

Several severe financial crises have started with some kind of financial innovation. To some extent, innovations promise to improve efficiency in the financial system, but ultimately they may also serve as a source of financial instability. For example, securitization and structured financial products received praise in the past; but after the global financial crisis of

2008–2009, we see clearly that there was a lack of understanding of how they shift risk and change the behavior of market participants.

Studying past episodes of financial instability and systemic risk is useful, not because we expect that they repeat themselves exactly, but because this helps to identify common features and sources, which then allow us to assess better the challenges that we face today. Now, for example, the rhythm of innovation in financial markets and intermediation is at unprecedented levels. Recent developments in information technology, such as the blockchain, machine learning, and artificial intelligence, have partly fueled this. One may wonder whether new products, such as crypto-currencies (Bitcoin, Ethereum, etc.), might be an important source of systemic risk so as to threaten the stability of financial systems worldwide.

Identifying common features of systemic crises throughout history is the first step toward controlling and minimizing its negative effects. In first part of this book, we look at the history of systemic crises and unify the different episodes of financial instability. In addition to innovation, we identify other common sources: common risk exposures, macroeconomic exposures, competitive pressure, poorly designed regulation, political influence, deregulation and liberalization, and interconnections/interlinks between financial intermediaries.

Once we identify a potential source of financial instability, measuring systemic risk is the crucial next step. Our presentation of historical episodes of financial instability identifies several channels that lead to practical measurement challenges. The first challenge is that systemic risk is multi-dimensional, so it may require focusing on particular aspects. Another challenge is that not all data may be available at sufficient frequency to provide reasonable estimates of systemic risk. Finally, another challenge is that systemic risk has both a temporal dimension and a cross-sectional one. It is difficult to address all these challenges in a single measure of (systemic) risk, so the measurement literature focuses on outcomes of systemic risk instead. In the second part of the book, we present several systemic risk measures that the literature introduced over the past ten years. In addition, we discuss the current situation worldwide using real data.

The first two parts of the book show that systemic risk is important qualitatively and quantitatively. Therefore, it may be efficient to intervene in the financial market to solve market failures leading to excessive systemic risk. In the third part, we discuss whether and how financial authorities should implement prudential actions. We stress that a purely micro-prudential perspective of financial regulators is necessary but not sufficient to control systemic risk. A broader (macro-prudential) perspective is required that encompasses the entire financial system. We describe a series of tools and regulations that have been proposed and (partly) implemented.

Most of the regulatory effort goes into measuring systemic risk and writing prudential rules into the legal framework. Unfortunately, this approach neglects an important topic: implementation of regulation. In particular, the institutional design of regulators is a topic that most academic studies have ignored in the past. There remains the question of how to arrange prudential regulations in a manner that maximizes the likelihood of timely and efficient use. The organization of the governmental agencies devoted to take care of systemic risk should ensure prompt, proactive actions once they identify vulnerabilities. In addition, their setup should provide the right incentives to all the involved parties and ensure accountability mechanisms. We present the analysis of an optimal institutional organization of financial regulation near the end of the book.

In summary, the book presents an overview of stylized facts, methods, and existing regulations. It provides a practical guide that should help those interested in systemic risk to identify potential sources, to assess their importance, to apply prudential actions, to decide on the way to implement them to promptly control the risk, and, if not successful, to resolve the problem with the lowest cost for society.

PART 1
History

Systemic risk and systemic crises have a long history, reaching (at least) as far back as the Tulip Mania in the 17th century.[1] This part presents cases of systemic bank crises, their trigger events, and their impact. We aim at understanding the different aspects of systemic risk and systemic crises.

Over the past 40 years, systemic risk has come to the forefront of regulatory and public attention. The increased importance of systemic risk is partly rooted in fundamental changes in the way banks operate now. Technological and financial innovations have changed their operations substantially; financial innovation in the form of securitization and derivatives trading have allowed new forms of sharing risks; and globalization has affected businesses and banks alike.

Over time, our understanding of systemic risk has changed. At the end of the 20th century, systemic risk was commonly addressed nationally and in the context of counterparty risk. It was often modeled via interbank linkages and/or allocation imbalances (see, e.g., Kaufman, 1995; Kaufman and Scott, 2003). The financial crisis of 2008, and most specifically the default of Lehman Brothers, has altered this perception fundamentally. Instead of modeling systemic risk itself, researchers now analyze how systemic risk spreads throughout the banking system and how minor events serve as amplifying factors. Thus, the focus has turned to the outcomes of systemic risk and the propagation and amplification effects.

Before the 21st century, systemic risk was mostly a national concern; but with the new century, systemic events reached the global level. Therefore, we split our historic overview in two parts. The first Chapter focuses on events at the end of the 20th century and highlights the systemic risk events in individual countries across the globe. The second Chapter then discusses global systemic events in the early 21st century. After this overview of historical systemic events, the third Chapter summarizes the main aspects and mechanisms of systemic risk.

---

[1]The Tulip Mania is a period in the Dutch Golden Age during which contract prices for bulbs of fashionable tulips reached extraordinarily high levels and then dramatically collapsed in February 1637. See Reinhart and Rogoff (2009), Bordo *et al.* (1995), Bordo (1990) and Brunnermeier and Schnabel (2015), among others, for additional information on historical (systemic) bank crises.

Chapter 1

Major systemic crises across continents at the end of the 20th century

This chapter presents a short overview of the international history of systemic risk in the 1980s and 1990s. To highlight its facets, we select particular systemic crises that occurred during those years. To show the international dimension of systemic risk, we look at systemic risk in both developing and developed countries. Our crises cover (all) different geographical regions (North America, Latin America, Europe, Asia, Australia, Middle East/Africa) and different mechanisms through which systemic risk manifests itself.[1]

A discussion of systemic risk before the global financial crisis is interesting because the experiences of developed countries is very different from those of developing countries. Systemic crisis events have been rare in developing countries, and the literature has largely ignored systemic risk. However, the literature on developing countries has considered systemic risk aspects long before the global financial crisis of 2008 (see, e.g., Tenconi, 1993; Daumont *et al.*, 2004; Honohan, 1993; Paulson, 1993).

We start with North America in the first Section, where we analyze the Savings & Loan crisis and the U.S. bank crisis that led to the failure of the Continental Illinois Bank and Trust Company (Continental Illinois). We then turn to Latin America and present the systemic crises in Chile and Mexico, along with the crises in Argentina and Uruguay at the beginning of the 2000s. In Europe, we look at the Spanish crisis of 1977 and the Nordic crises of the 1990s. This is followed by an overview of the Japanese crisis in the 1990s and the Asian crisis of 1997. We then address the Australian

---

[1]Our selection of individual crisis events includes only crises of the entire financial system. Thus, the failure of individual banks is considered a systemic event only when it is part of a larger (macro) systemic crisis. For example, we do not consider Drexel Burnham Lambert in 1990, Barings Bank in 1995, Long Term Capital Management in 1998, Enron in 2001, and Amaranth Advisors in 2006; see also Bullard (2008).

crisis in 1990, briefly present aspects of systemic events in African countries and then turn toward the Israeli bank crisis of 1983. Table 1.1 provides an overview of the crises discussed in this chapter.

1.1   North America

The 1970s were characterized by fundamental changes in the macro-economic environment, e.g., floating international exchange rates and increasing price levels due to oil shocks (see Federal Deposit Insurance Corporation, 1997, Chapter 1, p. 4). In the 1970s, the Federal Reserve Board raised short-term interest rates. Limits on deposit rates led to a financial innovation (money market funds) that offered higher returns than deposits. The withdrawal of funds from financial institutions created liquidity problems and decreased their profitability.

In addition, in the late 1970s, intrastate banking restrictions and regulations on deposit interest rates were lifted in the United States (e.g., through the Depository Institutions Deregulation and Monetary Control Act of 1980). The financial liberalization caused significant changes in bank business strategies, and some banks experimented with highly speculative investments and assumed excessive risks.

We discuss first the Savings & Loan crisis and look at the failure of the Continental Illinois Bank and Trust Company (Continental Illinois). The source of the first crisis lies in financial liberalization and deregulation, while that of the second lies in an aggressive growth strategy. Both crises were triggered by the United States recessions from January 1980 to July 1980 and again from July 1981 to November 1982.

Table 1.1: Overview of systemic crises at the end of the 20th century.

	Year	Crisis origins	Trigger events	Impact
North America				
Savings & Loan crisis	1980–1995	Similar business strategies, deregulation, financial liberalization	Interest rate changes	Almost a third of S&Ls closed or resolved
U.S. Bank crisis	1980s	Aggressive growth strategy	Recession	Large number of defaults; Continental Illinois too big to fail
Latin America				
Chile	1981–1983	Financial liberalization, credit expansion, capital inflows, weak banking supervisor	Currency devaluation, triggered by change in U.S. monetary policy	Nationalization of more than 50% of banking sector
Mexico	1994	Financial liberalization, credit expansion, capital inflows	Currency devaluation, triggered by political unrest	Fraction of non-performing loans increased from 5% pre-crisis to 15%
Argentina and Uruguay	2001–2002	Macroeconomic imbalances and financial fragility: dollarization	Changes on capital markets, leading to currency devaluation	In Argentina, sovereign default; In Uruguay, bank run on 45% of deposits

(*Continued*)

Table 1.1: (*Continued*)

Europe				
Spain	1977	Interlinkage with real sector, cluster risk, credit expansion	Recession	52 of 110 banks affected
Nordic crises	1990s	Deregulation, financial liberalization, real estate bubble	In Norway, oil price shock; In Finland: tightening of monetary policy and tax reform	Strong government interventions
Asia				
Japan	1990–1997	Deregulation, increased competition, credit expansion	Interest rate increase	Low number of defaults, but economic stagnation
Southeast Asia	1997	Credit expansion, overlending, debt issuance in US dollars	Interest rate increase, speculative currency attacks	Massive IMF intervention
Australia				
Australia	1989–1991	Financial liberalization, deregulation, credit expansion	recession	Default of two large banks
Middle East & Africa				
African	1980s	Political influence	Shock to the real economy	Government interventions
Israel	1983	Stock manipulation, misconduct	Currency devaluation	Collapse of banking system

1.1.1 The Savings & Loan crisis

One of the most severe U.S. systemic crisis occurred in the 1980s: the Savings & Loan (S&L) crisis. Savings & Loan institutions are not-for-profit institutions that take on short-term deposits to finance long-term assets, usually mortgages (see, e.g., Robinson, 2013). For S&Ls, the simple intermediation between depositors and borrowers was quite profitable in the 1950s and 1960s. But in the 1970s, the Federal Reserve Board raised short-term interest rates significantly. As regulations limited deposit rates, depositors shifted their money from S&L deposits to money market funds (a financial innovation at that time). In addition to the depositors' withdrawals, the interest rate increase caused a severe decline in the value of long-term (mortgage) loans. Since S&L institutions primarily gave out long-term loans, they lost a significant portion of their net worth through these interest rate increases (see, e.g., Robinson, 2013).

According to Robinson (2013), regulators were well aware of the losses in the S&L segment but lacked sufficient resources to deal with them.[2] Instead, regulators hoped that a deregulation of the business would allow S&L institutions to become profitable again and outgrow their losses.

In 1980, the U.S. government initiated a process of financial liberalization in the Savings & Loan sector by passing the Depository Institutions Deregulation and Monetary Control Act of March 1980. This act significantly broadened the business (opportunities) for S&L institutions and allowed them to engage in transactions similar to banks. Many institutions engaged in risky investments without having adequate risk assessment and/or risk management (see, e.g., Ely, 1993). As the Savings & Loan crisis dragged on, more and more losses accumulated, leading to a large number of either closed or resolved institutions.

The crisis ended in the early 1990s, when interest rates declined and the yield curve turned upward again (see, e.g., Federal Deposit Insurance Corporation, 1997). Between 1986 and 1995, a total of 1,043 of 3,234 Savings & Loan associations closed or were resolved by the Federal Savings and Loan Insurance Corporation or by the Resolution Trust Corporation (see, e.g., Federal Deposit Insurance Corporation, 1997, Chapter 4). The total cost of the Savings & Loan crisis is estimated at US-$160 billion, with US-$132 billion paid by taxpayers (see, e.g., Ely, 1993).

---

[2]Robinson (2013) states that it would have cost US-$25 billion to pay off insured depositors of failed Savings & Loan institutions in 1983. Yet, the deposit insurance fund at that time had a total value of US-$6 billion.

1.1.2   *Continental Illinois and the too-big-to-fail policy*

While systemic risk in the 1980s and 1990s is often associated with the S&L crisis, another banking crisis occurred in the United States during the 1980s. During this crisis, more than 1,600 banks closed or received financial assistance from the FDIC (see, e.g., Federal Deposit Insurance Corporation, 1997, Chapter 1).

Between 1976 and 1980, Continental Illinois engaged in an aggressive growth strategy that increased both the size and the riskiness of its loan portfolio. When the United States entered a recession in July 1981 that lasted until November 1982, a large number of banks failed. The resulting banking crisis also affected several large banks. In July 1982, Continental Illinois had been close to failure when Penn Square Bank collapsed. While Continental Illinois did not collapse itself, the default of Penn Square Bank caused severe problems in Continental Illinois' loan portfolio that continued for several months. In early May 1984, deposits of over US-$10 billion were withdrawn (see, e.g., Wall and Peterson, 1990; Carlson and Rose, 2016). Ultimately, Continental Illinois failed in 1984 when the bank could not obtain the renewal of short-term uninsured deposits.

At that time, Continental Illinois was among the ten largest banks in the United States, and almost 2,300 banks held deposits there or had loaned funds to the bank. Due to its size and its connectedness within the banking sector, Continental Illinois was the first institution to be officially considered too big to fail (see, e.g., Kaufman, 2003). The FDIC fully insured all creditors and depositors, as well as the parent holding company, and further provided new capital together with emergency loans (see, e.g., Yergin, 1991).

This decision symbolized a reversal in the FDIC's policy on addressing failing banks. Previously, the FDIC paid only a portion of the amount owed to uninsured depositors (see Federal Deposit Insurance Corporation, 1997, Chapter 7, p. 44). To prevent bank runs on other large U.S. banks, the FDIC decided to fully insure depositors and declared Continental Illinois as being *too big to fail*.

The policy of saving banks and financial institutions that were thought to be too big to fail remained in place until the Lehman Brothers default. During the 2007–2008 subprime mortgage crisis, most failing banks (such as Bear Stearns) were considered to be too big to fail and either received emergency liquidity (Fannie Mae and Freddie Mac) or were acquired by other financial institutions. While Lehman Brothers was perceived by the market as too big to fail, it was allowed to fail, which created turmoil among market participants (see, e.g., Paulson jr., 2010).

1.2 Latin America

During the 1980s and 1990s, several Latin American economies experienced significant capital inflows followed by a capital flight that brought these countries (close) to default and destabilized their banking systems. While numerous crises occurred in Latin American countries,[3] we choose to examine the systemic crises in Chile in the 1980s, in Mexico in the 1990s, and in Argentina and Uruguay at the beginning of the 2000s because all four countries share strong similarities and highlight the difficulties in identifying (increases in) systemic risk before a trigger event causes systemic crises.

The origins of these crises can be found in far-reaching financial liberalization, in fixed/pegged exchange rates in the cases of Chile and Mexico, as well as in financial fragilities (liability dollarization, ill-designed safety nets, and cross-border expositions) in the cases of Argentina and Uruguay. Significant capital inflows met a banking system that was ill prepared to handle a sudden supply of (cheap) money and that lacked regulatory supervision.

At first sight, the trigger event in these crises may be attributed to a change in the exchange rate, i.e., a macroeconomic shock affecting the whole banking system followed by a liquidity constraint. However, that exchange rate change was triggered by other events. In the case of Chile, the trigger was a change in U.S. monetary policy. In the case of Mexico, the trigger was an information shock in the form of political unrest. In the case of Argentina and Uruguay, the trigger was the failure to adequately address the currency–growth–debt trap into which these countries fell after devaluation of the Brazilian currency in January 1999.

1.2.1 *The Chilean crisis*

The origins of the Chilean crisis of the 1980s date back to the 1970s. During that decade, the Chilean government implemented a series of neo-liberal economic reforms including (financial) liberalization and privatization. To

---

[3] For a broad discussion of financial market fragility in Latin America, see Rojas-Suarez and Weisbrod (1994); for an overview of credit expansion and the mortgage sector, see Cubeddu *et al.* (2012) and Iakova *et al.* (2014). For more details about the Chilean and Mexican crisis presented here, see Edwards (1996).

achieve (comparatively) low levels of inflation, a fixed exchange rate regime with the U.S. dollar was installed in 1979; see, e.g., Barandiarian and Hernandez (1999), p. 12. Chile experienced a significant inflow of capital and commercial bank credit increased, see, e.g., Barandiarian and Hernandez (1999) and Margitich (1999), p. 39.

Risk management in banks did not adapt sufficiently to these structural changes (capital inflows, neo-liberal reforms, privatization of banks). Worse, Chilean banks in general faced limited incentives to implement adequate risk assessment strategies since the Chilean government had previously built a reputation of bailing out failing banks, e.g., SINAP in 1974 (Brook, 2000). Moreover, the banking supervisor (Superintendency of banks and financial institutions, SBIF) was weak, either through institutional weakening (depletion of resources and attributions), through the application of a formal supervision approach that was inadequate, and through deficiencies in the process of licensing and supervision of the risks. Hence lending standards decreased and the inflow of commercial credit increased lending, even to low-quality borrowers.

Considering the depreciating pressure on the U.S. dollar during the 1970s, the fixed exchange rate caused an overvaluation of the Chilean peso. Moreover, with its fixed exchange rate, Chile became increasingly dependent on U.S. monetary policy. When the U.S. dollar started to rise in 1980, capital inflows to Chile stopped and a recession started. In November 1981, the bank crisis became evident when two banks had to be bailed out by the government, with several minor banks following until early 1983 (Montiel, 2014, p. 32).

Downward price rigidity impeded a real depreciation of the Chilean peso. This created political pressure to devalue, so that in 1982 the fixed exchange rate regime was abandoned. A large nominal depreciation resulted, that affected the payment capacity of highly (external) indebted companies. This led to a systemic banking crisis. By 1985, 14 of 26 national banks and 8 of 17 financial institutions had been nationalized, i.e., the Chilean government owned more than 50 percent of the banking system (Brook, 2000, p. 76).

1.2.2   *The Mexican peso crisis*

In the 1980s, Mexico started a process of financial liberalization (major structural reforms, privatization, and deregulation). From 1989 onward, it had further adopted a crawling peg exchange rate to the U.S. dollar that ultimately led to an overvaluation of the Mexican peso in international currency markets; see, e.g., Griffith-Jones (1997), Turrent (2008), Edwards (1996).

The Mexican banking system was ill prepared to deal with the subsequent capital inflow (Graf, 1999). First, the regulation and supervision of Mexican banks was comparatively light. Second, the privatization process within the Mexican banking sector had structurally changed banks themselves and altered their business strategies (Edwards, 1996, Table 1). Mexican banks started to pursue an aggressive lending strategy from the end of the 1980s to 1994. Between 1987 and 1994, commercial bank credit grew by over 100 percent and consumption credit by more than 450 percent (Griffith-Jones, 1997). Bank credit to private enterprises was at about 10 percent of GDP in 1988 but grew to more than 40 percent of GDP in 1994 (Mishkin, 1996, Figure 3).

The capital inflow and the credit expansion were sustained by Mexico's international reputation as a successful reformer in Latin America (Griffith-Jones, 1997; Montiel, 2014). Yet, in 1994, the political and economic stability of Mexico was threatened by an upheaval of domestic violence that alienated international investors. To counter the start of the outflow of international capital, the Mexican government took on exchange rate risk; they issued short-term debt denominated in Mexican pesos with a guarantee for full repayment in U.S. dollars.

During 1994, the U.S. Federal Reserve raised interest rates in several small steps. Many international investors transferred their funds back to the United States. Mexico experienced a significant outflow of capital, and the central bank lost a substantial amount of reserves. When more than US-$4 billion of reserves were withdrawn around December 20, 1994, Mexico faced bankruptcy (Griffith-Jones, 1997, p. 21). On December 22, 1994, the central bank ultimately gave up the crawling peg of the peso to the U.S. dollar and allowed the peso to depreciate. The Mexican economy went into a recession, and companies facing insolvency meant that banks ended up with a large percentage of non-performing loans (Mishkin, 1996). The percentage of non-performing bank loans increased from less than 5 percent in 1991 to about 15 percent in 1995 (Mishkin, 1996).

1.2.3   *The Argentine and Uruguayan crises*

After decades of high inflation and successive failures in reducing it, domestic monetary policy in Argentina and Uruguay lacked confidence at the end of the 1980s. This led to an extended use of foreign currency, in particular the U.S. dollar, as a substitute for local currency in Argentina and Uruguay, a process commonly referred to as dollarization. During the 1990s, these countries implemented stabilization policies that used the exchange rate as a nominal anchor to domestic price dynamics. These policies did provide nominal stability and boosted financial intermediation, but they did not foster fiscal or monetary discipline.

In the case of Argentina, De La Torre *et al.* (2003) argue that the failure to adequately address the currency-growth–debt trap, into which the country fell at the end of the 1990s, precipitated a run on the currency, and the banks followed by the abandonment of the currency board and a sovereign debt default. Two major explanations have been given for the failure of the Convertibility Program (the currency board regime). Most observers relate the failure to the unholy combination of a fixed exchange rate and large fiscal deficits that led to a rapid growth in public debt, severe fiscal sustainability problems, and eventually a loss of access to the credit markets. Another view stresses the impact of a fixed exchange rate regime coupled with devaluation by Brazil, Argentina's major trading partner, in January 1999.

After the Asian crisis of 1997 and the Russian crisis of 1998, capital markets drastically changed their behavior. In particular, Calvo *et al.* (2003) argue that developments at the center of capital markets were key to producing an unexpected, severe, and prolonged stop in capital flows to emerging market economies. Argentina and Uruguay were no exception. Moreover, two structural characteristics of these economies, being relatively closed economies and liability dollarization, made them particularly vulnerable. Being a closed economy implies that a sudden stop in capital flows may call for a sharp increase in the equilibrium real exchange rate. Liability dollarization, in turn, entails foreign-exchange-denominated debt in non-tradeable sectors, which implies large balance sheet effects when the real exchange rate rises. Thus, these two factors represent a dangerous financial fragility through which a currency crisis may rapidly lead to a banking crisis.

As the collapse in Argentina became evident inside Uruguay, the first re-action of Argentine depositors was a "flight to quality," i.e., shifting deposits from the Uruguayan branches of Argentinian banks to other Uruguayan banks. However, after the enactment of the freeze of bank deposits in Argentina, Uruguayan banks started to lose deposits. At first, the run af-fected only those banks that were most exposed to Argentinian banks, but after some time, the bank run generalized. At the pinnacle of the crisis in

July 2002, it endangered 45 percent of total deposits. According to De Brun and Licandro (2006), despite the fact that some elements of contagion were present, the main explanation for the Uruguayan crisis involves financial fragility and a poorly designed regulation (which did not deter but foster currency mismatches), combined with the strong real exchange rate depreciation and spillover effects from the Argentinian crisis. In Uruguay, these elements led to a rational simultaneous run on both the domestic banking system and the public debt. In Argentina, the fixed exchange rate was abolished, the currency devalued, and the sovereign defaulted.

1.3   Europe

In the 20th century, several European countries experienced systemic bank crises. We choose to look at the Spanish crisis of 1977 and the Nordic crises of the 1990s. These two European crises are among the most severe systemic crises of the 20th century, according to Reinhart and Rogoff (2009).

The case of the Spanish crisis of 1977 highlights how a lack of diversification in business strategy can lead to the propagation of systemic crisis within a banking sector. The case of the Nordic crises encompasses several systemic crises in Scandinavian countries in the 1980s and 1990s. Here, we highlight the cases of Norway and Finland to show how financial liberalization and deregulation, together with credit expansion and inadequate risk management, can slowly build up systemic risk.

1.3.1   *The Spanish banking crisis of 1977*

During the 1960s, the Spanish banking sector was highly regulated, and the government intervened extensively in the financial system, e.g., through entry barriers or interest rate controls (Pons, 2002). Furthermore, bank resources were targeted toward economic and industrial priorities of the government. This strategy established a strong link between Spanish banks and the real economy.

From the early 1970s onward, a process of financial liberalization and deregulation started that fundamentally altered the Spanish banking sector. It allowed Spanish banks to expand their business but also increased competition within the banking sector. According to Martin-Acena *et al.* (2010), the expansion strategies of most Spanish banks were unprofitable.

Because of the strict regulation in the 1960s and early 1970s, banks held significant industrial portfolios and were tightly connected with the real economy. When the oil price shock of 1973 slowly altered the industrial environment (increasing labor costs, increasing energy costs, and higher inflation), banks faced a cluster risk in the real economy (Vives, 1990). In the mid-1970s, Spain entered a deep economic recession that increased the number of non-performing loans in the Spanish banking sector.

As inflation increased, nominal interest rates increased. Almost immediately, several smaller banks experienced liquidity shortage. This was initially covered by a limited guarantee for deposits, issued by the central bank. In November 1977, the Deposit Guarantee Fund was established, providing liquidity to failing banks and aiming at restructuring and reorganizing these banks.

Between 1977 and 1985, 52 of 110 banks were affected by the crisis; 24 banks had to be actively rescued; another 20 banks were nationalized; 4 were liquidated; and another 4 were forced into mergers. In total, these 52 banks encompassed about 20 percent of deposits within the Spanish banking sector at the time (Martin-Acena *et al.*, 2010, p. 38).

The case of the Spanish crisis of 1977 shows how a crisis in the real economy spills over to the banking sector. Here, the concentration in industrial portfolios and the respective cluster risk caused the propagation of the bank crisis. Still, it is important to recognize that this cluster risk was not necessarily caused by a sector-endogenous decision for similar business strategies but by an exogenous regulation that established and strengthened the linkage between the real sector and the banking sector.

1.3.2   *The Nordic crises of the 1990s*

The 1980s saw a strong movement toward financial liberalization in all Scandinavian countries: interest rates were deregulated, currencies were allowed to float freely, and the concurrent deregulation of banking presented new business opportunities. This process set off strong capital inflows that led to massive credit expansion and a boom in the real estate markets of all Scandinavian countries (Honkapohja, 2009; Jonung *et al.*, 2009).

Norway experienced high growth and a lending boom from 1983 onward (Vale, 2004). A real estate boom and high competitive pressure within the banking sector caused a lowering of credit and mortgage standards; banks started to give loans to high-risk investment projects and individuals.

In late 1985, the Norwegian economy was hit by a significant decline in oil prices. This macroeconomic shock changed the economic environment and led to interest rate increases. Several Norwegian banks started to feel the effect of a liquidity shortage, and from 1988 onward, several (mostly smaller) banks defaulted (Vale, 2004, p. 5). By late 1990, the remaining larger Norwegian banks were also under extreme pressure and close to default. For example, the second largest Norwegian bank had lost all of its equity. In this systemic crisis, the Norwegian Central Bank intervened and provided liquidity support and capital injections.

Finland was hit a few years later by a systemic crisis. Following the financial liberalization in the early 1980s, Finnish banks expanded their borrowing in foreign currency, which led to asset price increases and credit expansion (Honkapohja, 2009). Bank lending grew between 20 and 30 percent per year in Finland (Jonung *et al.*, 2009, p. 82). Risk management was not commensurate during this period of credit expansion. The net foreign debt as a percentage of the GDP increased from 17 percent in 1986 to 45 percent in 1990 and to over 60 percent in 1994 (Honkapohja, 2009, Table 3.1).

The central bank addressed these developments by tightening monetary policy. This slowed down bank lending in the late 1980s and, in particular, the use of short-term credit to finance long-term investments. A tax reform in 1990 added further pressure on the real interest rates by cutting the marginal tax rate on interest deductions. A large number of non-performing loans was revealed, which brought several banks close to default.

In fall 1991, SKOP, a mutually owned central institution of savings banks, collapsed due to a lack of liquidity (Jonung *et al.*, 2009, p. 85). Because of the high level of interconnectedness of SKOP with the savings banks, the central bank feared a contagious effect on the weakened Finnish banking system. It, therefore, decided to intervene by taking control of several banks and providing deposit guarantees. In 1992, the Finnish government created a bad bank for all toxic assets and gave out an initially zero-interest convertible loan of approximately EUR 1.2 billion to Finnish banks (Honkapohja, 2009).[4] Still, the crisis spilled over to the real economy. The total gross cost of the systemic crisis in Finland is estimated to present approximately 9 percent of Finland's GDP in 1997 (Honkapohja, 2009, p. 24).

---

[4]The other Scandinavian countries were hit by similar events. The Swedish currency came under attack by currency speculators in late 1992 (Jonung *et al.*, 2009, p. 59). While the events in Norway, Sweden, and Finland are subsumed under the name of the Nordic crises, there was no orchestrated policy to jointly deal with the crisis.

1.4   Asia

Several Asian countries experienced systemic bank crises toward the end of the 20th century. We choose to examine the Japanese bank crisis of the 1990s and the Asian crisis of 1997. Both crises are intertwined: While the Japanese crisis had been going on for most of the 1990s, banks only started to default in 1997 due to the additional pressure that came from the Asian crisis. Moreover, several authors (Corsetti *et al.*, 1999) argue that the severity of the Asian crisis of 1997 was influenced by the economic stagnation in Japan.

1.4.1   *The Japanese bank crisis of the 1990s*

In the 1990s, Japan experienced a severe and prolonged bank crisis, with several banks defaulting in 1997 and 1998. The crisis occurred at the end of a long-lasting stock market and property boom that was fueled by expansionary monetary policy.

Traditionally, the Japanese banking sector was characterized by three particular features. First, the sector was heavily managed by the Japanese Ministry of Finance, e.g., by limiting competition between banks and monitoring commercial loan rates. Second, banks focused on financing the growth of heavy industries. Third, they established long-term relationships with (large) corporations and provided the main source of their funding, even in difficult times (Baba and Hisada, 2002).

Following the Plaza Accord of 1985, the Japanese banking sector changed fundamentally. First and foremost, Japanese banks lost part of their traditional customer base as Japanese corporations gained better access to international capital markets. In addition, Japanese banks started to face competition from international (global) banks establishing subsidiaries in Japan. This loss in traditional customers and the increased competition made Japanese banks turn their focus away from heavy industries to other industries.

Following the expansionary policy of the Bank of Japan, the booming property sector promised high returns with land as (supposedly) safe collateral (Baba and Hisada, 2002; Shiratsuka, 2003). Over the years, Japanese banks pursued aggressive (over-)lending strategies in the construction and real estate sectors; for example, Nakaso (2001), p. 36, states that "profitability and riskiness of each loan were often neglected and loans were extended at negative lending spreads."

Soon, a massive asset price bubble built and the Japanese economy started to overheat. When the Bank of Japan started to raise interbank lending rates in 1990, real estate prices and asset prices in general started to decline. The construction and real estate sectors were particularly affected, leading to large amounts of non-performing loans on banks' balance sheets. Banks were unwilling to realize losses and kept these assets on their balance sheet (Espig, 2003; Kanaya and Woo, 2000, p. 23); according to Cassis (2011), p. 44, banks even continued lending to troubled and failing corporations.

Since the entire banking sector relied strongly on the real estate sector with highly overvalued assets, most Japanese banks in the system had to deal with declining asset values at the same time. The Bank of Japan feared (disorderly) defaults and subsidized illiquid banks, even those close to default (Hoshi and Kashyap, 2004). The bailout plan covered losses of more than 3 trillion Yen and initially prevented bank runs and losses to depositors.

However, the bailout plan also prevented the clean-up of the Japanese banking sector and kept many "zombie" banks alive, prolonging the crisis period. The bank crisis broke out in 1997, when the additional pressure of the Asian (currency) crisis let several Japanese banks fail, e.g., the Long-Term Credit Bank of Japan and the Nippon Credit Bank in 1998 (Espig, 2003).

1.4.2 The Asian crisis of 1997

In the 1980s and 1990s, many Southeast Asian economies developed into export-oriented economies. Growing exports fueled an investment boom in industrial assets, increasing production capacities. The wealth generated from exports fueled the construction and real estate sectors within these economies (Hunter *et al.*, 1999; Ariff and Khalid, 2000).

In the mid-1990s, the macroeconomic environment started to change. In particular, the U.S. economy started to recover from a recession, and U.S. interest rates increased. This led to a strong appreciation of the U.S. dollar versus other leading currencies. Due to pegged (in some cases crawling) exchange rates of Southeast Asian countries, their currencies appreciated, too, causing a loss in export competitiveness.

To make matters worse, Japan, as a main trade partner of these countries, experienced a period of economic stagnation (Corsetti *et al.*, 1999). Previous massive investments had generated excess capacities. Market pressure now caused falling prices and decreased companies' profitability while still leaving them with large debt repayments (Agenor *et al.*, 1999).

The Asian crisis began in February 1997 in Thailand with the default of a large property developer. This default "revealed" that several Thai property developers were close to default and fueled market fears of a widespread chain reaction of defaults in the Thai economy. Due to strong inter-linkages between the real estate and banking sectors, the dire situation of property developers posed a threat to the stability of several large banks. In particular, Finance One, the country's largest financial institution, seemed to be in trouble as it had issued a large amount of bonds in U.S. dollars and used the proceeds for loans to property developers. Now that property developers could not make their payments, Finance One had difficulties in making its own payments on the bonds issued (Mansharamani, 2011, Chapter 9).

In May 1997, short sellers attacked the Thai baht, and in June 1997, the government had to let the currency float. The success of the currency attack on the Thai baht introduced a wave of other attacks on countries in the same situation. In July 1997, Malaysia and Singapore gave up their currency pegs to the U.S. dollar; Indonesia followed in August 1997. All these countries had experienced excess investments with high borrowing (predominantly in U.S. dollar-denominated debt). In the second half of 1997, currencies such as the Thai baht and the South Korean Won lost about 50 percent toward the U.S. dollar, and local stock markets fell by up to 50 percent (Goldstein, 1998, p. 3).

These events affected Asian financial institutions in at least two ways. First, before the crisis, banks had issued U.S. dollar-denominated debt to refinance loans that were provided in local currency. This had allowed them to benefit from lower interest rates in the U.S. as long as the currency peg remained. But once the currency peg vanished, the interest income generated in local currency no longer sufficed to cover the bond payments necessary in U.S. dollars.

Second, local banks had practiced over-lending in the previous years. Bank lending to the private sector had increased substantially on an annual basis (generally in the double digits) and represented more than 50 percent of the local GDP in 1996 and 1997 (Corsetti *et al.*, 1999, Tables 18 and 19). However, they had not applied adequate risk assessments with loans. When the real economy experienced a loss in competitiveness and declining revenues, banks faced a large number non-performing loans.

Despite its widespread impact on the region and the strong currency devaluation, this was only slowly identified as a crisis event. For example, in November 1997, at the Asia Pacific Economic Cooperation Forum in Vancouver, Bill Clinton, U.S. president at that time, still considered the Asian crisis to represent "a few small glitches in the road" (Goldstein, 1998, p. 1).

1.5 Australia

Australia has experienced several severe bank crises over the past century, e.g., the crisis of 1977 with the failure of the Bank of Adelaide (Stanford and Beale, 1987). We focus on the bank crisis of 1989–1991 in Australia (Gizycki and Lowe, 2000) because it provides an example how competitive pressure within the banking sector and the lack of supervision can lead to a systemic bank crisis.

The Australian banking sector experienced significant financial liberalization and deregulation in the 1980s, e.g., the abolishing of interest rate controls. In the course of this deregulation, Australian banks could expand their business across Australian states and overseas. At the same time, foreign banks were allowed to enter the Australian market. These developments greatly increased the competitive pressure within the Australian banking sector. Banks were in strong competition for market share and balance sheet growth, and this pressure further increased after the stock market crash of 1987. To maintain market share, Australian banks focused on the booming property sector and lowered their standards for mortgages. Thereby, they took on high risk in the commercial property market (Gizycki and Lowe, 2000, p. 183).

In 1990, Australia was hit by a major recession with a large increase in unemployment rates (1989: 6.1 percent; 1992: 10.7 percent). The recession also triggered a decline in property prices, and the low credit quality in most banks became evident. The share of non-performing loans increased substantially and ultimately caused the failure of two large Australian banks, the State Bank of South Australia and the State Bank of Victoria.

The State Bank of South Australia had previously over-focused on asset growth and had given out loans without adequate risk assessment. The bank failed in early 1991 and received a capital injection of more than AUS-$3 billion from the Australian government.

The State Bank of Victoria shared a similar fate. Originally a savings bank with some commercial banking, it had used the deregulation of the 1980s to form a merchant bank subsidiary, Tricontinental. This subsidiary was severely hit by non-performing loans and accumulated losses of more than AUS-$2 billion. The State Bank of Victoria failed in 1991 and was ultimately merged with another Australian bank, see Sykes (1994, p. 437).

1.6   Africa and Middle East

On the African continent, we focus on developments in Cameroon and Ghana. We then turn to the Middle East and look at the Israeli bank crisis of 1983 since it represents a prime example of the long-lasting and self-fueling build-up of systemic risk.

1.6.1   *Systemic crises in African countries*

African countries have experienced a multitude of (systemic) bank crises. Daumont *et al.* (2004) discuss ten individual banking crises that occurred between 1985 and 1995. They highlight the strong interrelation between the banking sector and the government and classify the ten banking crises into three categories linked to particular channels: (1) the operating environment, e.g., limits on diversification or exogenous shocks; (2) the market structure, e.g., the form of bank ownership or banking concentration; (3) bank conduct, e.g., bank competition or governance structures.

In Cameroon, banks were legally required to have at least a third of their capital come from the government. This requirement gave the government a significant influence in bank decisions and imposed a strong link between banking and politics (Daumont *et al.*, 2004, p. 28). Regulation, thus, limited the diversification opportunities of banks and instead induced a cluster risk in all Cameroonian banks.

The impact of this political influence in banking became evident in several crises. For example, in the 1980s, Cameroon experienced a severe bank crisis following a downturn in the economy. Banks in Cameroon faced a large percentage of non-performing loans (60 to 70 percent of outstanding loans according to Daumont *et al.*, 2004, Table 1). Due to the over-reliance on specific sectors in the economy and a lack of diversification, the country's commercial bank and two development banks were technically insolvent in 1987.

In Ghana, the government intervened in the banking sector by influencing the credit allocation. Guidelines determined this allocation in the form of maximum increases in loans to individual sectors. These maximum increases were set individually for each sector, depending on its priority for the government. These guidelines increased the similarity in business strategy and credit allocation of banks in the country. This turned into a significant disadvantage during the bank crisis of the 1980s (1982–1989). Following an economic decline, banks were faced with a large percentage of non-performing loans (40 percent of credit to non-government borrowers).

The experience of most African countries shows that the political influence in banking and the resulting overlending to specific industries (regardless of other investment opportunities) cluster risks that accumulate systemic risk.

1.6.2 The Israeli bank crisis of 1983

The Israeli bank crisis represents a systemic crisis following fire sales in the stock market. The crisis has its origins in stock price manipulations and the associated mis-allocation of capital as well as in misconduct; see (Kedar-Levy, 2016) for a detailed analysis).

The Israeli bank sector was (and still is) highly concentrated, with just a small number of large Israeli banks and very few foreign banks operating in Israel. The Israeli banking sector was tightly linked to the Tel Aviv Stock Exchange (TASE), since the exchange was initially founded by commercial banks and companies specializing in securities trading. The board of the TASE and its committees were dominated by bank representatives; consequently, banks determined their own rules.

When the public became interested in the stock market in the early 1970s, several banks began "influencing" their own share prices at TASE by investing in their own shares via mutual funds and pension funds under their management. This practice artificially increased the share price and, thus, the stock return (Blass and Grossman, 1996; Kedar-Levy, 2016, p. 85). Over several years, different strategies of artificial stock price increases were pursued more and more aggressively, leading to significant overvaluation of bank shares. In the early 1980s, bank shares generated an average return of more than 25 percent annually (Prager, 1996; Blass and Grossman, 2001).

The bubble burst in August 1983 when the Israeli government announced a devaluation of the local currency (Shekel) by 8 percent and hinted at additional future devaluations. With a loss in the currency value, investors started to transfer funds to dollar-denominated accounts. The substantial sales in bank stocks caused equity losses in Israeli banks that culminated, in early October 1983, in a share price crash of commercial banks. On October 6, 1983, TASE ceased operation for two weeks.

By the end of 1983, the largest banks had lost more than 50 percent of their value. By 1993, the bank sector was completely state-owned (Prager, 1996, p. 229).

Chapter 2

Major systemic crisis in the 21st century

Technological and financial innovation, as well as the globalization of business, have had a huge impact on banks. From the late 1990s onward, the interconnectedness of banks and the competition within the banking sector have significantly increased on a global level; see, e.g., Kroszner (2000). Different from the crises in the 20th century, systemic crises in the 21st century have no longer been confined to individual countries but have a strong international, even a global, dimension.

This chapter discusses the history of systemic risk in the 21st century. Because of the international dimension of banking, we organize it around crisis events and not around individual countries. First, we look at the global financial crisis of 2008–2009. We discuss events in the United States, in particular, in the U.S. housing sector, and look at spillovers to other countries. Specifically, we address the situation in Iceland, which lost its complete banking sector in the global financial crisis. We then present the second major systemic crisis in the current century: the European sovereign debt crisis that affected many European nations.

2.1 The global financial crisis

2.1.1 The subprime crisis & the fall of Lehman Brothers

In the U.S., the 1990s and early 2000s were characterized by a movement toward financial deregulation (Baker *et al.*, 2005, pp. 37–39) that greatly broadened banks' business opportunities. For example, the 1999 repeal of the Glass-Steagall Act of 1932 revoked the strict separation of investment banks, commercial banks, and insurance brokerages and allowed the creation of universal banks in the United States.

Starting in March 2001, the U.S. experienced a recession; to fight this recession and the economic impact of the 9/11 attacks, the Federal Reserve lowered its interest rate from 6% in January 2001 to 1.75% in December 2001. The interest rate was kept at a very low level until 2004.

Low interest rates fueled a booming housing sector and allowed people to obtain higher mortgages. Housing prices in the United States appeared to be ever increasing, so the investment in real estate seemed to be affordable not only because of the low mortgage payments, but also because of the strong appreciative pressure in the real estate value itself.

Banks extended their involvement in the mortgage sector and in the subprime mortgage sector in particular. Two elements encouraged this. First, in the low interest rate environment at that time, the subprime mortgage sector promised higher returns and looked considerably more attractive than in normal times. In addition, the underlying real estate properties promised to be safe collateral with lasting value, i.e., risk was often perceived as lower than it actually was. Second, securitization gave banks new business opportunities. Banks switched to a business model in which loans were provided with the intention of selling them off to financial markets later, the so-called "originate-to-distribute" business model. Since banks now had less intention of keeping the mortgages on their own books, they granted more mortgages to risky (subprime) borrowers. While this shift did not necessarily affect the riskiness of a bank, it changed the riskiness of structured products (securitizations). Structured products were opaque, and investors may not have taken these changes into account properly.

In 2004 and 2005, the Federal Reserve then increased its funds rate again, and the U.S. housing sector started to slow down in 2006. With a slowing economy and increased interest rates, homeowners were less able to fulfill their mortgage obligations, particularly in the subprime mortgage segment. As more real estate properties went into foreclosure, their prices further declined, starting a vicious cycle of decreasing real estate prices and increasing number of mortgage defaults.

In 2007, the global financial crisis started.[1] (For a full timeline of the financial crisis, see, e.g., to the Federal Reserve Bank of St. Louis at https://www.stlouisfed.org/financial-crisis/full-timeline.) In February

---

[1]In hindsight, one may wonder why these events were not identified at the time. Reinhart and Rogoff (2008), p. 3, describe that in the early 2000s, the strong increases in the U.S. housing market were thought to be justified by financial innovation (in particular, securitization) and capital inflows, i.e., the increases in the U.S. housing market represented an elevation of growth and, thus, wealth. While there were some warning voices (Roubini, 2006), the majority of market participants did not believe the housing market would be a foundation for a future (systemic) crisis.

2007, Freddie Mac stopped buying the most risky subprime mortgages, and in April 2007, New Century Financial Corporation was the first leading subprime mortgage lender to file for Chapter 11 bankruptcy protection. In the summer of 2007, the problems in the U.S. housing market and subprime mortgage sector became evident when rating agencies started to downgrade subprime mortgage bonds and Bear Stearns had to liquidate two hedge funds involved in this market segment.

Since structured products were opaque, the influence of defaults on individual market participants was not commonly known. The high level of uncertainty and the lack of information on the actual risk distribution made risk-averse investors refrain from further investment. Banks turned to liquidity hoarding as a protection against counterparty risk and the illiquidity of assets. Funds in the money market strongly decreased in summer 2007; see, e.g., Heider *et al.* (2015) for an analysis of counterparty risk during the global financial crisis. In fall 2007, premiums on credit default swaps (CDS) sharply increased and the commercial paper market shut down.

While many market participants were still hoping for a simple market correction, 2008 revealed the intensity and extent of the subprime mortgage problem. In spring 2008, Carlyle Group failed to meet margin calls on its mortgage bond funds, and in March 2008, Bear Stearns had to be taken over[2] by JP Morgan Chase. But Bear Stearns was not the only company to fail in the subprime crisis. In June 2008, Bank of America acquired Countrywide Financial Corporation; and in the summer 2008, Fannie Mae and Freddie Mac came under intense market pressure so that the Federal Reserve Board had to authorize lending to both institutions. The U.S. Securities and Exchange Commission (SEC) prohibited naked short selling in the securities of Fannie Mae and Freddie Mac. Still, both institutions were placed under government conservatorship on September 7, 2008.

The crisis peaked in September 2008, when Merrill Lynch and Lehman Brothers ran into serious refinancing troubles. On September 15, 2008, Merrill Lynch was acquired by Bank of America, but Lehman Brothers had to file for Chapter 11 bankruptcy protection.[3] The very next day, the (mortgage) insurer AIG was taken over by the Federal Reserve for US-$85 billion, and on September 17, 2008, the SEC announced a temporary

---

[2]Bear Stearns had been heavily involved in securitization and the issuance of asset-backed securities. When investors experienced the first losses in these markets, Bear Stearns increased its exposure expecting a quick rebound in valuation. When prices continued to fall, the company failed and was acquired by JP Morgan Chase.

[3]For a detailed description of events, see Paulson jr. (2010), Sorkin (2009), and Ball (2018).

emergency ban on short selling in all financial stocks. On September 25, 2008, JP Morgan Chase acquired the banking operations of Washington Mutual; and on September 29, 2008, Citigroup announced its purchase of the banking operations of Wachovia Corporation (which was later acquired by Wells Fargo in a competing offer).

The Lehman failure led to a loss of confidence in the global financial system as Lehman Brothers had previously been considered to be *too big to fail*. At that time, Lehman was the fourth largest investment bank in the United States; the market perception was that if Lehman was not *too big to fail*, then no bank may be. This led the market to a significant reassessment of default probabilities.[4]

The loss of confidence within the banking sector was so severe that banks stopped lending to each other in early October 2008. The illiquidity of credit derivatives, such as mortgage-backed securities, amplified the crisis; these products could not be sold and valuation could not be marked-to-market as there was no longer any market for the products. Since the risk distribution in the U.S. banking sector was obscured by the use of derivatives, risk-averse investors assumed the worst, e.g., they considered all business partners to potentially have an exposure to Lehman (Chakrabarty and Zhang, 2012).

The response to the liquidity shortage was the Troubled Asset Relief Program (TARP), announced on October 14, 2008. Therein, the U.S. Treasury Department offered a total amount of US-$250 billion in capital to U.S. financial institutions.

2.1.2 *The global dimension*

The interconnectedness of banks allowed the crisis in the U.S. market to spread to other countries. The complexity of international bank products increased the level of uncertainty internationally and changed the perception of risk. In previous years, investors had seen strong growth with low volatility, had started to ignore risk, and instead had formed a firm belief

---

[4]This development is surprising considering the origins of the term *too big to fail* and the situation of Continental Illinois in 1984. Back then, the interconnectedness of Continental Illinois was a main point for the intervention; in 2008, Lehman Brothers was thought to be less relevant in size. Several authors have hinted at the default of Lehman Brothers preventing a potential moral hazard within the markets (Ball, 2018), meaning that no individual bank should be able to count on the bailout. However, in hindsight, the high level of interconnectedness of Lehman Brothers, particularly in the CDS market, allowed the default of a single institution to propagate globally and to amplify in many markets.

in ever-increasing stock markets. They supposed that risk was successfully reduced by better diversification thanks to new financial products (e.g., mortgage-backed securities).

U.S. mortgage-backed securities were selling in international markets, i.e., the (subprime) risk of the U.S. housing sector was distributed on a global level. This international dimension became evident almost immediately in the (liquidity) situation of Northern Rock, one of the largest mortgage lenders in the UK. The bank's main business strategy had consisted of borrowing substantially in international money markets in order to fund mortgages. In 2007, the income from these mortgages significantly decreased, and Northern Rock was unable to make its own payments. In this situation, the bank sought help from the British government in the form of liquidity support, which was granted in September 2007. However, the request for liquidity support triggered a bank run on Northern Rock as depositors feared the bank to be close to bankruptcy. In February 2008, Northern Rock was taken into state ownership.

Following the severe systemic events in U.S. markets, investors started to re-evaluate their investments. At the same time, international banks were affected by the liquidity shortage in global markets and the illiquidity of credit derivatives. Laeven and Valencia (2010) analyze the global dimension of the global financial crisis of 2008. Their Table 1 presents a list of countries experiencing a systemic crisis in 2007 and/or 2008. They report 13 systemic bank crises in Austria, Belgium, Denmark, Germany, Iceland, Ireland, Latvia, Luxembourg, Mongolia, Netherlands, Ukraine, United Kingdom, and the United States. In addition, the authors identify 10 "borderline cases" in France, Greece, Hungary, Kazakhstan, Portugal, Russia, Slovenia, Spain, Sweden and Switzerland.

The crises identified by Laeven and Valencia (2010) highlight the truly international dimension of the global financial crisis. The total cost of restructuring national financial sectors was approximately 5 percent of national GDP; between 2007 and 2011, public debt increased by around 24 percent of GDP. These severe costs contributed to the outbreak of the European debt crisis.

During the global financial crisis of 2008, one single country experienced the largest relative loss in total bank assets: Iceland. There, the events in the United States triggered the crisis that would wipe out almost all banks. Relative to the total assets of defaulting banks (representing about 90 percent of assets of all banks), the Icelandic bank crisis of 2008 constitutes the largest systemic banking crisis (Laeven and Valencia, 2010, p. 17).

2.1.3   The systemic crisis in Iceland

In the early 2000s, Iceland had successfully diversified its economy into manufacturing and services. The deregulation and privatization of Icelandic banks initiated a further expansion of the banking sector (see, e.g., Aliber and Zoega (2014)). This expansion was financed via the interbank lending market (as the domestic market was comparatively small) and, subsequently, by attracting (mostly short-term) capital from abroad by offering higher interest rates than other European banks. Credit creation was channeled to the construction sector, initiating a sharp asset price increase in real estate; the higher demand was linked to a higher demand for mortgages. Household debt built up substantially and reached 220 percent of disposable income at the end of 2007, according to data from the Organization for Economic Cooperation and Development (OECD).

When the financial crisis erupted in 2007–2008, the macroeconomic environment changed, with short-term lending drying up and limiting the ability to rollover loans. In addition, the Lehman default altered the perception of risk/uncertainty, and investors soon perceived Icelandic banks to be riskier than previously thought.

Wholesale funding dried up in September 2008 after internal documents of Glitnir, one of the largest Icelandic banks, had been leaked, revealing the large external debt of Icelandic banks. On September 29, 2008, it was announced that Glitnir would be nationalized on October 7, 2017. On that same day in October, Landsbanki (the largest Icelandic bank) was placed under government receivership, followed by Kaupthing Bank on October 9, 2008. The Financial Supervisory Authority took control and—to prevent bank runs—turned domestic deposits into priority claims, and new banks were founded to take over the domestic operations of the failing banks. Furthermore, the government guaranteed all domestic deposits in (new) Icelandic banks (Aliber and Zoega, 2014).

In the case of Iceland, the sheer size of the banking sector made a government intervention (bailout) impossible. In mid-2008, the three failing banks had assets in excess of ISK 14 trillion, more than 10 times the Icelandic GDP. The Central Bank of Iceland was unable to serve as the lender of last resort. The three Icelandic banks may have been considered too big to fail, but they eventually turned out to be too big to rescue. This provides an interesting twist on the too-big-to-fail policy.[5]

---

[5]The Luxembourg banking sector was also too big to be rescued for this small nation. There, the two biggest private banks, Dexia-BIL and Fortis, could only be saved by

2.2 The European sovereign debt crisis

The global financial crisis had a strong and long-lasting impact on international markets. Several countries experienced financial turmoil; the perception of the United States altered as ratings were lowered following the raising of the public debt ceiling in August 2011; and the perception of the Euro area changed from a single economic unit to a more dis-aggregated view of individual countries differing in riskiness. Several European countries were characterized by large (some even excessive) deficits and faced difficulties in refinancing their government debt. Greece was one of the first countries experiencing such difficulties; Ireland, Portugal and Spain were particularly hard hit; but there were also tensions within the Italian financial sector.

The Greek banking sector had previously experienced a financial boom decade (Pagoulatos, 2014, p. 453). Historically, the Greek banking sector was highly concentrated and state controlled, but it was privatized from 1995 onward. After joining the Euro area in 2001, Greece experienced the benefits of a stable currency with comparatively low interest rates (Marsh, 2009). (The interest rate for 10-year bonds was 6.1% in 2000 and fell to 3.5% in 2005; in comparison, the interest rate on German 10-year bonds was 5.2% in 2000 and 3.3% in 2010.)

These lower borrowing costs supported a rapid credit expansion in subsequent years. Between 1990 and 2006, total bank output increased, on average, by 6.6 percent annually (according to Athanasoglou *et al.*, 2008)).[6] For example, between 2001 and 2006, the household savings rate fell from +3.2% to −3.2%. The decrease in interest rates also enabled the government to borrow at lower interest rates, increase its financial flexibility, and increase Greek sovereign debt. By 2009, the net foreign debt was at 86 percent of GDP (European Economic Advisory Group, 2011, p. 109).

On February 5, 2010, the Greek government corrected its budget deficit; it requested financial support from the European Union on April 11, 2010 (Rocholl and Stahmer, 2016). Over the following weeks, more and more negative information about Greece was revealed. For example, on April 22, 2010, the EU updated the estimated 2009 deficit for Greece from

a concerted action of the Luxembourg and the Belgian governments. Preventing outsized banking sectors is nowadays a regulatory concern; see e.g., actions by the Swiss government.

[6]We focus here on changes in savings, debt, and credit that are important for the financial sector, but there are several causes for the Greek economic crisis; see, e.g., Tsoulfidis *et al.* (2016).

12.7 percent to 13.6 percent and further announced that the deficit might ultimately be beyond 14 percent (Augustin *et al.*, 2016). The slow dissemination of information actually increased uncertainty about the future of investments in Greek sovereign debt. Investors feared Greece to be in worse shape and that the bailout program might not suffice.

The biggest fear was a Greek (unstructured) default that would lead to contagion between banks on a global level. While Greek banks held a major part of Greek sovereign debt, Greek sovereign debt had been widely traded among banks, and many European banks also had significant exposure to Greece. For example, in 2010, French, Swiss and German banks held more than EUR 75 billion, EUR 64 billion, and EUR 43 billion of Greek sovereign bonds, respectively.

There were several reasons to fear reactions. First, this event occurred shortly after the global financial crisis and banks' balance sheets had not yet (fully) recovered. A further hit might have threatened the stability of several European banks, with potential contagious effects on a European and global level. For the link between the commonality in asset holdings and the fear for contagious effects following a Greek default, see, e.g., Allen *et al.* (2012a). Second, the Greek default would have triggered payments on CDS contracts. Since these contracts are traded globally by investors with and investors without direct exposure to Greece, the effect on individual market participants was unknown. This further increased the perceived level of uncertainty.

On May 2, 2010, the Euro area countries and the IMF bailed out Greece with EUR 100 billion. This bailout was supposed to calm financial markets and lower uncertainty. However, according to the analysis by Augustin *et al.* (2016), it had the opposite effect and caused an increase in Greek CDS spreads (from 337 bp to 697 bp). The first bailout, finalized in May 2010, was followed by a second bailout program of an additional EUR 172.6 billion in March 2012. In April 2012, a 50 percent haircut on bank-held sovereign bonds was implemented (Vogiazas and Alexiou, 2013). Since the bailout was also linked to strict austerity measures, the Greek economy experienced a severe contraction and subsequent rise in unemployment [Monokrousso *et al.* (2016)].[7]

But Greece was not the only country to experience difficulties in refinancing government debt. At the end of 2010, Ireland had to apply for

---

[7]While other bailed-out countries in Europe also had to implement austerity measures, Greece remained the epicenter of protests against the bailout and austerity measures, fueling investors' uncertainty about future Greek economic decisions.

aid from the European Union and the IMF as well, worth several billions of euros (Lane, 2012). In exchange for this bailout, the Irish government presented spending cuts and tax hikes to reduce the budget deficit over the following years. The Irish bailout was officially announced on November 28, 2010, and encompassed 85 billion euros. In the following weeks, the borrowing costs of countries like Spain and Italy increased and pressure on these governments intensified. In the spring of 2011, several rating agencies downgraded Portugal, such that it had to seek a financial bailout from the European Union on April 6, 2011; see, e.g., De Santis (2012). This bailout was officially approved on May 16, 2011, with the money coming from the European Financial Stabilization Mechanism, the European Financial Stability Facility, and the IMF.

The European Sovereign Debt Crisis lasted at least until 2014, when Ireland and Portugal were able to exit their bailout programs, and Greece regained (partial) access to capital markets.

Chapter 3

Common features in the history of systemic crises

The previous chapters presented several systemic crises over the last five decades. We have identified several characteristics of systemic risk. This chapter will provide a short review of the common features in systemic crises.

3.1 Systemic crises at the end of the 20th century

As Savings & Loan institutions traditionally followed the same business strategy without any significant diversification (opportunities), an external shock changing this market environment negatively affected all institutions. The reasons behind the Savings & Loan crisis may be seen in this similarity of business strategies. In the 1970s, the increase in interest rates on money market funds together with the financial innovation served as a shock that destroyed the profitability of S&L business strategies.

The crises in Latin America highlight the macroeconomic (shock) aspects of systemic risk. Both Chilean and Mexican crises are exemplary for the systemic risk mechanism of a macroeconomic shock and the additional exchange rate risk that developing countries face. The Chilean crisis can be traced back to a systematic shock to banks that turned into a systemic event: the external macroeconomic shock of an interest rate increase in the United States altered the market environment for all banks in the Chilean banking system (to different degrees). The capital flight from Chile worsened the liquidity situation for banks at large and, furthermore, negatively affected the economy. The fixed exchange rate regime was abolished and a systemic crisis started. In the cases of Argentina and Uruguay, macroeconomic imbalances and financial fragility, due to liability dollarization and poorly designed prudential regulation, implied a significant real exchange rate depreciation that, in turn, led to simultaneous run on both the domestic banking system and the public debt.

The Australian crisis of 1991 shows how competitive pressure within the banking sector can actually build the foundation for a systemic crisis. While each bank individually sought to increase market share, the joint effect was a lowering of risk standards and an (unrecognized) accumulation of credit risk. Because regulation and supervision had not yet adapted to the financial liberalization and deregulation movement of the 1980s, this risk accumulation was not addressed, and the recession could ultimately serve as the trigger for the bank crisis. The propagation and amplification of the Australian bank crisis occurred via the loan market.

Poorly designed financial regulation plays a peculiar role in systemic risk. In the Israeli experience of the 1983 crisis, a lack of regulation and widespread fraudulent behavior (stock price manipulation) were the origins of the crisis. Similarly, the Asian crisis of 1997 is rooted in over-lending to the private sector. The easy access to a large supply of liquidity fueled excess growth that soon generated over-capacities. The changing macroeconomic environment (e.g., increase in U.S. interest rates) ultimately triggered the crisis by revealing structural imbalances.

Different from that, the experience of African countries shows that strong political influence and over-regulation in banking may facilitate the accumulation of systemic risk. When regulation is not focusing on risk management but is influenced by political incentives, banks may take on cluster risks on their balance sheets that they are not allowed to diversify for political reasons. A negative shock to the real economy then negatively affects all bank balance sheets and endanger the stability of the banking system.

Systemic crises may also be rooted in a process of financial liberalization and deregulation.[1] We have seen this in the Nordic crises of the 1990s. After financial liberalization, financial institutions also pursued highly similar business strategies, exposing them to similar risk (and macroeconomic shocks). The high level of interconnectedness of the mutually owned central institution of savings banks, SKOP, can be considered an example for being too interconnected to fail (Jonung *et al.*, 2009, p. 85). The main source of the Japanese crisis lies in financial liberalization (1985 Yen-Dollar Accord) and the excessive credit expansion in the real estate sector and mortgage market, leading to similar risk exposures.

---

[1]For a detailed discussion of the linkage between financial liberalization and systemic risk, see Kaminsky and Reinhart (1999).

All the 20th century systemic crises that we presented had a strong impact on the banking sector within the respective country, but they did not spread much across borders. The Asian crisis at the end of the 20th century is an exception since it spread across various countries. In retrospect, this crisis may be seen as the first systemic crisis of a new kind that became prevalent from there on. While the idea of systemic risk and the spreading of financial crises had long been addressed in the economic literature, Bartram *et al.* (2007) state that the real starting point for research on contagion was the Asian crisis of 1997 (Calvo and Mendoza, 2000; Kodres and Pritsker, 2002; Dungey *et al.*, 2005).

3.2 Systemic crises of the 21st century

In the 20th century, we saw strong interconnectedness across borders only in the Asian crisis of 1997. Since then, banking activities have become more and more global, and securitization has facilitated the trading of assets (and risks) globally. Looking at systemic crises in the early 21st century, we see that the global dimension and spreading of crisis events greatly intensified.

While our presentation in the previous Chapter has stressed the worldwide dimension, the global financial crisis of 2008 is in many ways similar to previous financial crises that countries experienced in the previous century. It fits into classic boom-bust episodes following financial liberalization: With increasing asset prices, banks lowered their reliance on deposits and instead diversified toward wholesale assets that are less stable but promise higher returns. The crisis of 2008 also fits into the category of systemic crisis following financial innovation, here in the form of securitization. Several authors have linked it to financial deregulation. For example, Acharya *et al.* (2011), p. 2, state that "the past decades of liberalizing markets, removing regulatory restrictions, and trusting markets to discipline themselves have had the unintended consequence of destabilizing the financial system."

The availability of cheap money, the low interest rates, and the re-packaging of risk (though securitization) contributed to financial imbalances. Furthermore, the intended diversification of risk increased the interconnectedness of banks, making them more vulnerable to systemic shocks. Few authors, such as White (2006), had seen the risk of these global imbalances. The 2008 financial crisis suddenly revealed the fragile foundation of the global financial system to most market participants.

The World Finance Summit held in London in April 2009 also identified several contributing factors to the global financial crisis: inadequate risk management (e.g., high leverage, misleading ratings), misaligned incentives through remuneration schemes, and fraudulent behavior by individual employees (G-20, 2009). In hindsight, the interconnectedness of banks and the fluidity of global savings can be considered propagating factors during the crisis. Amplifying factors were the illiquidity of markets, mark-to-market valuation, and the excessive leverage of banks.

The global financial crisis certainly contributed to the European debt crisis as several governments had to spend large amounts for the restructuring of the financial sector. This added to the respective deficits, and when the dire situation in Greece became public, investors lost their trust in European governments and their ability to refinance their debt. The European debt crisis, thus, shows how a systemic bank crisis can spread to the sovereigns and become contagious on the macroeconomic level.

3.3   Main historical insights

Over the course of the last 50 years, we have identified several sources of systemic crises. In the last century, we have seen a major role played by common risk exposures (similar business strategies in the case of S&L, macro exposures in the case of Chile and Mexico), dollarization (Argentina and Uruguay), competitive pressure (Australia), poorly designed regulation (Israel and the Asian crisis), and political influence (Africa), among other causes.

One recurrent theme throughout is the role of deregulation and liberalization. The majority of historical crises are preceded by financial liberalization, as documented in Kaminsky and Reinhart (1999). It played a role in the S&L crisis, the U.S. bank crisis following the default of Continental Illinois, and the crises in Chile and Mexico in Latin America. One may subsume deregulation and liberalization under a general heading of poorly designed financial sector oversight. Then, one can also attribute directly the Argentinian and Uruguayan crises as well as the subprime/GFC crisis, in addition to those attributed above to poorly designed regulation.

Innovation, is another recurrent theme that plays a prominent role in many systemic crises. In the S&L crisis, it was the financial innovation of money market funds. Technological changes have made business and banks more global, leading to a globally integrated financial sector. Whereas crises were contained at the national level at the end of the 20th century, the beginning of the current century has seen the first truly global crisis of the global financial system. A major financial innovation (securitization) played a major role in the run-up to the global financial crisis, the subprime crisis.

Technological as well as financial innovation have changed fundamentally the way banks operate and how they interconnect and act internationally. This change has created unprecedented inter-linkages at the international level. In turn, this has created a global financial system with associated systemic risks. The new century has seen how these risks propagate and materialize in a global financial crisis.

Jordà *et al.* (2018) study the synchronization of financial cycles across 17 advanced economies over the past 150 years and show that the co-movement of credit, equity, and house prices has increased above and beyond growing real sector integration. The sharp increase in the co-movement of global equity markets in the past three decades is particularly notable. They also show that U.S. monetary policy has come to play an important role as a source of fluctuations in risk appetite across global equity markets.

Beyond these common features, there are some general historical insights to be gained. First, the Continental Illinois bank crisis shows that systemic risk in the form of propagation throughout the banking system was a concern long before the global financial crisis. However, until the Lehman Brothers default, the perception was that a failing bank would receive emergency liquidity, and market participants were calmed. Second, the Chilean and Mexican defaults show the difficulties in identifying systemic risk. In hindsight, Mexico followed the same path that Chile had taken a decade before, and it is evident that Mexico was heading for a similar systemic crisis as Chile.

Historical insights may help to identify sources of systemic risk. According to Reinhart and Rogoff (2008, 2009), qualitative and quantitative regularities across a number of standard crisis indicators are stunning. For example, the significant run-up in U.S. equity and housing prices prior to the global financial crisis looks like that of an archetypical crisis country in the last part of the 20th century. Based on a broad sample of banks from 17 OECD countries between 1987 and 2015, Brunnermeier *et al.* (2017) show that asset price bubbles in stock and real estate markets raise systemic risk at the bank level. Kaminsky and Reinhart (1999) find that these two variables are the best leading indicators of crisis in industrial countries experiencing large capital inflows post-World War II. Again, Reinhart and Rogoff (2008, 2009) find that the United States was on the typical trajectory, with capital inflows accelerating up to the eve of the crisis.

According to Jordà *et al.* (2011), the correlation between current account imbalances and lending booms has grown much tighter in recent decades. By studying the experience of 14 developed countries from 1870 to 2008, they conclude that credit growth emerges as the single best predictor of financial instability. Moreover, credit growth tends to be elevated and natural interest rates depressed in the run-up to global financial crises. Schularick and Taylor (2012) also find that credit growth is a powerful predictor of financial crises. They show that total credit has increased relative to output and money in the second half of the 20th century, suggesting that policymakers ignore credit at their peril.

The historical evidence presented by Brunnermeier and Schnabel (2016) suggests that the emergence of systemic risk episodes is often preceded or accompanied by an expansionary monetary policy, lending booms, capital inflows, and financial innovation or deregulation. Moreover, the severity of the economic crisis following the bursting of a bubble is directly linked to its financing. More precisely, crises are most severe when accompanied by a lending boom and high leverage of market players and when financial institutions themselves are participating in the buying frenzy.

Similar results are reached by Gourinchas and Obstfeld (2012): A key precursor of twentieth-century financial crises in emerging and advanced economies alike was the rapid buildup of leverage. Those emerging economies that avoided leverage booms during late 20th century also were most likely to avoid the worst effects of the 21st century global financial crisis.

PART 2
Measurement

This part discusses measurement of systemic risk. As we have seen in Part 1, systemic risk has many facets through which it affects not only the financial system, but also economic activities in general. Measuring risk of the entire financial system is of particular interest to financial regulators and, as such, is a good starting point to assess the impact of systemic events. Throughout, therefore, we focus exclusively on risks to the financial system.

Threats to the financial system come from (isolated) distress of individual banks. These risks are the topic of risk management systems in financial institutions and are the concern of financial regulators who intend to make them "safe and sound" individually (micro-prudential regulation view). As our history in Part 1 shows, previous crises, e.g., the global financial crisis of 2008–2009 (GFC) have considerably broadened our perspective; there are aspects to the financial system that go beyond the risks of individual institutions. For example, similar investment strategies in subprime credit appeared to be of little concern from the perspective of individual banks but created a herding that exposed banks to a similar shock. A holistic view of the entire financial system has emerged that looks at threats to the stability of the financial system as a whole (leading to a macro-prudential view).

In measuring systemic risk, there are many aspects that matter in measuring that risk and characterizing the details of the measures. In the first chapter in this part, we begin with how definitions of systemic risk evolved over time and end with our definition that drives measurement throughout Part 2. The next chapter includes economic concepts, desirable features of systemic risk measures, and a reference of several measures. This leads us to the third chapter, in which we discuss in detail the major risk measures and their implementation. Finally, in the last chapter, we implement these measures and provide an extended discussion of worldwide systemic risk in the current millennium.

Chapter 4

Defining systemic risk

In Chapters 1–3, we have shown that systemic events have common features across time and how a globalized financial system in the new century has created new challenges. Accordingly, the definition of what constitutes systemic risk has evolved over time. This chapter presents an overview of systemic risk and its evolution.[1]

Systemic crises have a run-up, a trigger, and a crisis phase; see, e.g., Brunnermeier and Oehmke (2012). During the run-up phase, individual banks and the entire financial system become fragile due to financial liberalization, deregulation, over-reliance on specific sectors/industries, excessive credit expansion, or real estate bubbles. Misconduct, political influence, macroeconomic decisions, such as the reliance on pegged exchange rates, contribute to systemic fragilities. (The history in Part 1 of this book provided examples of these in the previous century.)

Initially, systemic risk was assessed directly through measures based on the individual fragilities. The drawback is that these measures address only the fragilities under consideration. Therefore, early on, the literature focused on events during the crisis phase. During this phase, systemic risk shows up via (at least) three channels: (large) macroeconomic shocks, domino defaults, and imbalances in risk allocation (Kaufman and Scott, 2003; Trichet, 2009). These channels were most commonly used before the global financial crisis (GFC) to define systemic risk, and we discuss these in Section 4.1. After the GFC, attention has shifted to the outcome of systemic risk; we discuss this in Section 4.2.

---

[1]For further reading, see Oosterloo and de Haan (2003), who provide an overview of systemic risk definitions prior to the 2008 global financial crisis, and Smaga (2014), who focuses on systemic risk definitions after the 2008 crisis.

4.1   Channels of systemic risk

4.1.1   *Macroeconomic shocks*

Large macroeconomic shocks originate outside the financial system and affect all institutions within it, often transmitted via the real economy. For example, systemic risk can arise from a commonality in bank business strategies or activities that come from holding government securities (sovereign default risk).

While macroeconomic shocks occur in developing and developed countries, developing countries face higher risks as they receive capital flows that are large compared to their economies. In addition, shocks can spread more easily in these economies due to structural and institutional weaknesses, mismanagement, and misconduct. For example, when emerging countries peg their currency to the U.S. dollar, changes in U.S. interest rate policy (re-)direct international capital flows, which have a severe impact on developing countries and their banking systems. This impact is most evident in the Chilean peso crisis, see Section 1.2.1. In addition to currency pegs, we have seen that political influence has given rise to systemic risk in various African crises; see Section 1.6.1. Bank misconduct is at the root of the Israeli crisis of 1983, see Section 1.6.2.

Historically, macroeconomic imbalances built up in the pre-crisis stage and created financial fragility. Macroeconomic shocks turn vulnerabilities into a systemic event that first hits the economy then affects the financial system. Associated definitions of systemic risk relate directly to the underlying macroeconomic shock under consideration.

4.1.2   *Domino defaults*

Whereas the previous definition focuses on exposures to macroeconomic shocks, the concept of domino defaults considers the interconnectedness of banks. When banks are highly interconnected (e.g., through the interbank market), the default of bank A imposes a loss on the balance sheet of its counterparties, say on the balance sheet of bank B. When these losses are large, they endanger the stability of bank B. With each additional bank default, the pressure on the other banks within the system increases.

However, it has long been recognized in the bank run literature that both actual business exposures and perceived exposures lead to domino defaults. Since a bank default induces a (partial) loss to depositors, even rumors about bank instability can initiate a bank run (see, e.g., Diamond and Dybvig, 1983). When a bank has already experienced losses, the additional withdrawal of deposits worsens its liquidity situation and actually turn into a self-fulfilling prophecy. Since depositors expect the bank to (be likely to) default, they withdraw their deposits, thereby worsening the liquidity situation and increasing the default probability.

The development of international banking since the 1980s has increased the level of interconnectedness among banks (see. e.g., Aglietta, 1996) and lengthened the chain of direct exposures that are affected by a single event (bank failure). While classic lending relations between banks explicitly determine the impact of an individual default on other banks, after securitization became popular in the 1990s, products, such as credit default swaps, lead to an individual bank default affecting other market participants even without direct exposure.

In the 1990s, the term systemic risk was often linked to chain reactions of default. In 1994, the Bank for International Settlement defined systemic risk via the chain reaction of defaulting banks: Systemic risk is "the risk that the failure of a participant to meet its contractual obligations may in turn cause other participants to default with a chain reaction leading to broader financial difficulties" (Bank for International Settlements, 1994, p. 177). Kaufman (1995), p. 47, also states that "systemic risk is the risk of a chain reaction of falling interconnected dominoes."

4.1.3 *Imbalances in risk allocation*

Section 4.1.1 stated that banks may be exposed (knowingly or inadvertently) to a macroeconomic shock. One can view this as an imbalance in the risk allocation to that shock. However, banks' exposure to risk can be imbalanced more generally. Modern banking strongly depends on wholesale funding and securitized lending, which expose a bank to many different forms of risk. Banks could be unaware of (imprudent) risk imbalances that are due, for instance, to common exposures or to common business strategies that become apparent only in times of crisis.

For example, when a shock reduces the asset prices in a particular market, the resulting loss of a bank has a severe impact on leveraged banks. These banks might decide, or be forced, to sell some of their assets, but they are constrained by the liquidity situation of other banks. Their sales add further tension to the system, particularly during a crisis; when all banks follow similar business strategies, they are likely to be affected by the same shocks and also experience a loss at about the same time (to different degrees). Hence, industry peers might not be in the market as (first-best) buyers when a bank has to sell assets. Instead, assets are sold to other investors (second-best buyers) at lower prices (see Shleifer and Vishny, 1992). Fire sales further decrease asset prices and increase volatility (see Shleifer and Vishny, 2011).

When investors assume that all banks are affected by losses, they reduce their exposure. This fuels the downward pressure on bank asset prices. Less informed investors become unwilling to provide funding to leveraged investors and, instead, hoard their funds in risk-free assets, leading to a flight to quality and safety (Brunnermeier and Oehmke, 2012).

At the same time, the spread between assets with high and low liquidity increases, and investors consequently prefer to hold very liquid assets. Investors are willing to pay ever higher prices for these supposedly safe assets, trying to get into the asset class. Hence, a flight to liquidity starts.

Overall, as banks try to get out of risky assets (fire sales) and into safe assets (flight to quality), the banks' liquidity can also be negatively affected by lenders' flight to liquidity.

The more banks are perceived to be similar to defaulting banks or banks already in trouble, and the higher the level of perceived uncertainty, the more likely it is that market participants will withdraw funds and limit their exposure. For example, this was the case after the default of Lehman Brothers in 2008, when investors did not differentiate between banks with an exposure to Lehman and those without any (direct) exposure (see Chakrabarty and Zhang, 2012). Banks were (typically) unaware of a build-up in the system such that the actual (imbalances in) risk allocations surfaced only during the crisis.

4.2   Outcomes of systemic risk

It is difficult to enumerate all potential imbalances in financial markets that affect the financial system and use such a list to define systemic risk. Given the complexity, a more promising approach is to focus on the outcome (e.g., of any imbalances) during the crisis period and focus on similarities. After the experience with the 2008 crisis, the understanding of systemic risk changed, driving the literature to focus on the outcome of systemic risk[2]. For example, Anand and Schwarcz (2016), p. 9, define systemic risk

---

[2]In the 1990s, one of the few broad definitions of systemic risk is the "disturbance in financial markets which entails unanticipated changes in prices and quantities in credit or asset market, which lead to a danger of failure of financial firms, and which in turn threatens to spread so as to disrupt the payments mechanism and capacity of the financial system to allocate capital" (Davis, 1992, p. 117).

as "a possibility of financial meltdown that affects an entire economic system." This definition does not focus on how systemic risk spreads through the banking system; instead the definition focuses on its impact on the functioning and, thus, stability of the system.

In their analysis of historic systemic crises, Reinhart and Rogoff (2009) identify a crisis to be systemic if either of the following occurs: (1) bank runs that lead to the liquidation or the restructuring of one or more financial institutions, or (2) in the absence of bank runs, the closure, restructuring, or large-scale government assistance of one or more institutions that marks the beginning of similar outcomes for other financial institutions. In a similar manner, e.g., Demirgüc-Kunt and Detragiache (2002) and Demirgüc-Kunt and Detragiache (2005) consider an event to be one of systemic distress when at least one of the following occurs: (1) large-scale nationalizations; (2) emergency measures to support the banking system, such as bank holidays, guarantees, etc.; (3) cost of rescue operations of at least 2 percent of GDP; or (4) non-performing loans as a fraction of total loans are at least 10 percent.

The outcome that characterizes a systemic crisis should be adequate to the banking system under consideration. Caprio and Klingebiel (1997) and Daumont *et al.* (2004) focus on (4) above and define a systemic banking crisis when non-performing loans are at least 5 to 10 percent of total assets, arguing that this percentage is likely to wipe out most or all of the banking system's capital. This argument depends, however, on the fraction of non-performing loans that become reperforming later and on the losses incurred otherwise. For example, over the entire last decade, more than 5 percent (at times more than 10 percent) of loans in Italy were non-performing.

Laeven and Valencia (2010), p. 6, define a systemic crisis as a bank crisis that meets two conditions: significant signs of financial distress in the banking system (as indicated by significant bank runs, losses in the banking system, and bank liquidation) and significant banking policy intervention measures in response to significant losses in the banking system.

Castro and Ferrari (2012) state that systemic risk "broadly speaking is the risk of a widespread crisis in the financial system." Puzanova and Duellmann (2013) consider systemic risk to represent "the risk of a collapse of a financial system that entails a social welfare loss." Smaga (2014) uses the following definition of systemic risk: "the risk that a shock will result in such a significant materialization of (e.g., macro-financial) imbalances that it will spread on the scale impairing the functioning of financial system and to the extent that it adversely affects the real economy (e.g., economic growth)." Trichet (2009) states of systemic risk, "In the context of our economic environment, it is the threat that developments in the financial system can cause a seizing-up or breakdown of this system and trigger massive damages to the real economy."

To the best of our knowledge, there is still no unified definition of the term "systemic risk." In our understanding, systemic risk is best defined by focusing on its outcome(s) and not its transmission channels. We view risks to the stability of the financial system as systemic risk, i.e., we are concerned with stability of the financial system as a whole.

Our definition of systemic risk considers the financial system as an entity in itself. It focuses on aspects of the entire financial system that go beyond its being the sum of its parts. This distinction is reflected in prudential regulation. The so-called micro-prudential perspective intends to make individual banks safe and sound; the so-called macro-prudential perspective aims at risks to the entire financial system; the goal is to make the entire system safe and sound.

Chapter 5

Characterizing systemic risk

We start our discussion of systemic risk measures with broad economic concepts that influence this form of risk. This prepares the ground for systemic risk measurement in Section 5.2. Finally, Section 5.3 provides an overview of measures based on market data.

5.1 Economic concepts

5.1.1 *Propagation*

Systemic risk materializes when a shock hits the financial sector. Classical finance theory distinguishes systematic shocks, which affect all (or a large number of) asset values at the same time, from idiosyncratic shocks (unsystematic shocks), which affect the value of a single asset (or a small number of assets).

To become vulnerable to a specific systematic shock, banks must take similar risks such that they become exposed to that particular shock. From a conceptual perspective, one may think of banks taking identical investment strategies or investment strategies that are strongly correlated; see Acharya (2009).

One would then think of systemic shocks being closely related to systematic shocks. While this is true (see the historical events presented in Part 1 and our discussion in Chapter 4.1, there are more facets when one thinks in terms of outcomes. For example, systemic events can also be liquidity driven. A prime example is bank runs leading to a bank panic. After the introduction of deposit insurance, this has been considered a problem of the past in developed markets, but the run on the bank Northern Rock in Great Britain before the GFC and the runs on Cypriot banks in the Euro crisis are forceful reminders to remain vigilant about this risk in retail banks. Gale and Bhattacharya (1987) and Brunnermeier and Oehmke (2013) rationalize banks' reliance on short-term funding that exposes them to liquidity risk on the liability side.

Analogous problems come from the asset side. For example, fire sales by a bank depress the prices of assets, making further sales necessary. Mark-to-market accounting contributes to fire-sale contagion when forced sales depress prices, leading to the need for additional deleveraging; see Laux and Leuz (2010). Diamond and Rajan (2005) study how early liquidation may lead to reduced aggregate liquidity. Brunnermeier and Pedersen (2009) study "loss spirals" from margin requirements, see also Gorton and Metrick (2012). Heider *et al.* (2015) identify a form of a market break-down, which can lead to liquidity hoarding. Overall, the global financial crisis has been a forceful reminder of the importance of addressing liquidity since liquidity-driven runs in the interbank and repo markets have been a major factor in that crisis.

From a conceptual perspective, one can view the shocks to individual banks as idiosyncratic shocks. Micro-regulation treats these shocks in isolation: making banks safe and sound should make the financial system safer. However, the fallacy that this strategy makes the system safe became most evident during the global financial crisis.

The pioneering work of Allen and Gale (2000) and Freixas *et al.* (2000) shows that interbank relationships are subject to a phase transition. Idiosyncratic shocks can be shared efficiently through interbank relationships as long as they are sufficiently small, but these same relationships collapse the entire financial system once the shock size crosses a critical threshold. While their analysis focuses on the distinction between complete versus incomplete networks, Acemoglu *et al.* (2015) study more general networks; they confirm the phase transition and elaborate strongly on the mechanism for propagation of shocks to other banks.

Before the GFC, Allen and Gale (2000) and Freixas *et al.* (2000) already point for a way for individual shocks to become systemic. After the GFC, the literature began analyzing this in greater detail. It points out the importance of propagation mechanisms to understand systemic risk. For example, propagation effects can turn idiosyncratic shocks into systemic shocks over time. Such propagation effects come in two forms, contagion and amplification effects. Contagion effects characterize how a shock affects the entire banking network through their interconnections and how the shock leads to the default of a large number of banks (Allen and Gale, 2000; Freixas *et al.*, 2000; Elsinger *et al.*, 2006). Measures should therefore focus on default. Amplification effects study transmission channels through which an initially small shock becomes amplified so much that it threatens the financial system (Brunnermeier and Pedersen, 2009; Greenwood *et al.*, 2015; Duarte and Eisenbach, 2013). To measure the associated systemic risk, we should take into account a systemic risk measure that also looks at size in addition to default.

Several authors have studied networks in greater detail[1]. Nier *et al.* (2007) investigate banking networks by simulating changes. Eisenberg and Noe (2001) provide a methodological framework for analyzing interbank claims; in their framework a shock propagates and converges to a so-called fixed-point which then provides a way to study the ensuing systemic impact of the shock. Billio *et al.* (2012) use Granger causality to infer the network topology of hedge funds, banks, broker/dealers, and insurance companies. They find that networks are highly dynamic and became more densely interconnected from 1994–1996 to 2006–2008. Glasserman and Young (2015) estimate the extent to which interconnections in the Eisenberg and Noe (2001) framework increase expected losses and defaults under a wide range of shock distributions; estimates are based on data from the 2011 stress test conducted by the European Banking Authority for large European banks.

The Credit Research Initiative (CRI) at the Risk Management Institute of the National University of Singapore provides a publicly available ranking of systemic importance for exchange-listed banks and insurers around the world. This ranking uses the term structure of default probabilities developed by Duan *et al.* (2012), that is provided publicly through the CRI. Chan-Lau *et al.* (2018) build on the default correlations model of Duan and Miao (2016); they develop an algorithm and a mapping procedure to assess the systemic importance of more than 2,000 banks in their worldwide banking network.

While it is important to understand the channels through which a shock affects the financial system in a critical way, the current literature studies different channels largely in isolation. Moreover, feedback effects between the financial sector and the economy are largely left out. It would be desirable to build a general equilibrium model of the financial sector *and* the economy that permits analysis of systemic risk in a unified way. Ultimately, such a model could tell the researcher and regulators of an equilibrium response to shocks without undue reference to particular channels. Some progress has been made by Brunnermeier and Sannikov (2014), and the

---

[1] Allen and Babus (2009), Glasserman and Young (2016), and Neveu (2018) provide surveys of the financial network literature.

literature is growing. However, it is far from providing a rigorous, yet practical way of measuring systemic risk, which is the focus of this Part 2.

5.1.2   *Temporal and cross-sectional aspects*

The history of financial crises documents an important temporal dimension of systemic risk: financial crises do not arise suddenly; the underlying systemic risk builds up over time. Reinhart and Rogoff (2008) show historically that there are consistent leading indicators of banking crises; for example, they document asset price bubbles, corresponding credit booms, and large capital inflows into the economy. Laeven and Valencia (2013) come to similar conclusions. Macroeconomic measures, e.g., credit growth or the credit-to-GDP ratios, are in this category of intertemporal build-ups. For example, Schularick and Taylor (2012) study financial crisis in 14 countries from 1870–2008 and find that credit growth is a powerful predictor of financial crises. More generally, systemic risk can be seen in the build-up of financial imbalances, which can be inferred from the ratio of private credit to GDP, from growth rates in lending, from changes in property prices, asset prices or leverage(Borio and Lowe, 2002; Adrian and Shin, 2010).

In addition to the macroeconomic conditions are associated with the intertemporal build-up in systemic risk, there is also a risk management aspect. Banks take more (less) risks when volatility is low (high), and this has been attributed to risk management systems, in particular, Value-at-Risk (to be introduced in Section 6.1). This dynamic leads to an intertemporal build-up in risk taking that Brunnermeier and Sannikov (2014) classify as being excessive and refer to as the "volatility paradox."

As the literature has documented the temporal aspects of systemic risk, there have been attempts to model it. For example, models of contagion are introduced to the credit risk field by Davis and Lo (2001) and Jarrow and Yu (2001). Duan and Zhang (2013) study default cascades. Giesecke and Kim (2011) model temporal aspects through stochastic processes. However, assumptions on the underlying (continuous-time) process dynamics in such models are hard to justify, so the robustness of conclusions is unknown. Discrete-time GARCH processes, well-known in the financial literature, turn out to be useful, however, and the next chapter presents the SRISK approach of Brownlees and Engle (2016) building upon these.

Systemic risk is concerned about health of the entire financial system, so it makes sense to focus on aggregate properties of the system. Nevertheless, the system is composed of individual banks, so it is important to see *how* they aggregate to the system, i.e., to look at the cross-section of banks.

From a cross-sectional perspective, regulators can increase financial stability either by increasing banks' resilience, their ability to fend off the impact of other banks, or by decreasing their contagiousness, their ability to "infect" other banks. This is reflected in two ways through which the systemic risk contribution of a particular bank can be measured. The first considers adding the bank to the system and looking at the associated change in systemic risk. This approach addresses system resilience and has been pursued by, among others, SES/MES/SRISK, presented in Section 6.2 and Exposure-ΔCoVaR, presented in Section 6.1. The second way consists of measuring the change in systemic risk when that particular bank is affected by a shock (potentially distress); this approach addresses contagiousness and has been pursued by, among others, ΔCoVaR, presented in Section 6.1.

5.2   Features of systemic risk measures

The previous Section suggests that systemic risk has many different facets, so more than one single measure is necessary; see also Bisias *et al.* (2012). It is important to be transparent about the choices of measures. Regulators should be aware of both advantages and disadvantages of any measure; they should know what is (and is not) covered by a particular measure and what can (and cannot) be inferred. Understanding the limits can also provide the impetus to develop measures that target specific applications.

The advantage of measures that address particular economic channels is the ease with which they can be measured and the ease with which potential policy actions can be taken. The drawback, however, is that they rely on a particular economic mechanism, while history tells us that systemic risk usually does not come from the same angle again. This suggests being (partially) agnostic on the origins of systemic risk and focusing on unifying properties of crises and channels.

Modeling the outcome of systemic risk, instead of the channels through which systemic risk proceeds, is a convenient, practical way to address systemic risk. Our measurement approaches in Chapter 6, pursue probabilistic and statistical aspects, leading us to study measurement from an econometrician's perspective. The remainder of this chapter outlines several aspects and potential modeling choices of this approach that will guide us.

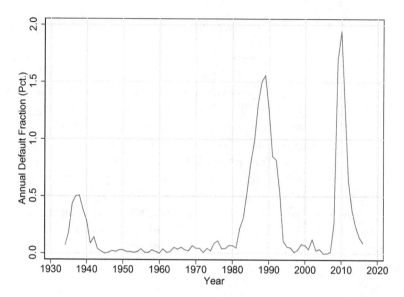

Fig. 5.1: Time series of annual default fraction among FDIC banks.

5.2.1   *Measurement object*

Insolvency of a bank, a primary concern of regulators, is a risk that can never be completely eliminated despite all risk management efforts. Instead of aiming to eliminate insolvency, a more reasonable objective is to keep insolvency risk at an acceptable level. Analogously, from the perspective of the financial system, a reasonable goal is to keep tabs on the fraction of banks that default at any point in time. Thus, the target variable could simply be the fraction of such defaults.[2]

Figure 5.1 presents the yearly fraction of banks that default among those insured through the Federal Deposit Insurance Corporation of the U.S. The time series runs from 1934 to 2016; the average is 0.2% across all those years. (The great depression of the 1930s saw a large fraction of banks default in any given year but is not covered.) In this annual time series are three major peaks: at the end of the 1930s, at the end of the 1980s, and the global financial crisis of 2007–2008 (GFC). The default rate during the GFC reaches (almost) 10 times the average annual default rate. Figure 5.2 presents the density of the default fraction (plotted up to 2%), derived

---

[2]Somewhat related to this, Ahnert and Georg (2018) define systemic risk as the joint default probability of banks.

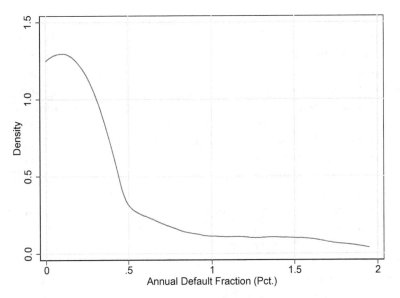

Fig. 5.2: Histogram of annual default fraction among FDIC banks.

through a kernel density estimation (Epanechnikov kernel with bandwidth 0.2%). It is highly skewed and stretches out far to the right; observations up to almost 2% are not uncommon. Overall, Figures 5.1 and 5.2 show that the default fraction is an important aspect of systemic risk.

We assume the banking system contains N banks and index them by $i = 1, \ldots, N$. We then define the default frequency M_N by setting

$$M_N = \frac{1}{N} \sum_{i=1}^{N} X_i, \text{ where } X_i = \begin{cases} 1 \text{ , default} \\ \\ 0 \text{ , otherwise} \end{cases} . \qquad (5.1)$$

M_N is a random variable that describes the fraction of banks that default and takes values of $\frac{i}{N}$; $i = 0, \ldots, N$.

In looking at the fraction of default, we treat all banks equally, whether small or large; this can be extended by adding the size of banks. But without further modifications, this extension assumes implicitly that the entire bank value would be lost, which is not the case in practice. An extension would have to model the losses-given-default (LGD), which requires a careful distinction among the seniority of claims, most notably between equity- and debt-holders. The literature does not follow this extension route; instead, it models directly associated changes (losses) to assets and, ultimately, to equity.

At the heart of the micro-prudential perspective on prudential regulation are the Basel Accords. These regulatory rules require (solvent) banks
to keep a minimum of (regulatory) capital, the amount set in relation to
risk-weighted assets. Banks have to report the relevant (audited) accounting information on a regular basis and must be closed when the minimum
capital is no longer available. (Likewise, non-financial firms are insolvent
from a balance sheet perspective when the firm does not have enough assets to pay all debts, i.e., when equity is negative.) While this approach
addresses banks individually (micro-prudential perspective on the bank system), it appears reasonable to measure the capital excess (or shortfall) of
the entire financial system from a macro-prudential perspective.

We consider the temporal evolution of banks over time and denote by
natural numbers s the respective dates at which accounting information
becomes available. For each bank $i = 1, \ldots, N$ and each possible date s, we
then denote by A_{is}, D_{is}, E_{is} the (book) value of assets, debt, and equity at
date s. The balance sheet closes, i.e., $E_{is} = A_{is} - D_{is}$. Figure 5.3 illustrates
our notation of accounting values.

Throughout, we consider banks that are traded on public exchanges.
For these, the market value of equity is available but on a much higher
frequency, e.g., daily instead of quarterly. We denote these market values
by V_{it}, see Figure 5.3 for an illustration.

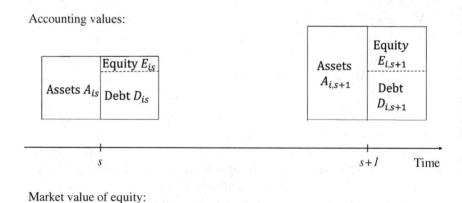

Fig. 5.3: Temporal evolution of accounting and market values.

The literature studies both absolute and relative changes; it considers changes both in asset and in equity values. In the interest of keeping notation as simple as possible throughout the measurement part of this book, we denote all these by the letter R. With respect to asset values, we use one of the notations $R_{is} = A_{i,s+1} - A_{i,s}$ for absolute changes, $R_{is} = (A_{i,s+1} - A_{i,s})/A_{i,s}$ for relative changes, or at times $R_{is} = \log(A_{i,s+1}/A_{i,s})$ for asset changes, all between some date s and the next date $s + 1$. (The logarithm is a convenient, common transformation that leads to a distribution on the entire real line.) Alternatively, we use analogous notation with both book and market equity values replacing asset values. It will always be clear from the context what definition we refer to.

5.2.2 *Expectation and conditioning*

Risk measures assess future developments of a financial parameter; in particular, systemic risk measures assess future developments of the financial system. Such an assessment requires a probabilistic model of future events to the measurement object. From a conceptual viewpoint, we treat future values as random variables that are characterized by a probability distribution; we denote by $P[\cdot]$ the probability measure describing the events in the banking system and by $E[\cdot]$ the associated expectation operator.

To be precise, at a date, say s, the current values of the assets, debt, and (book) equity are known, but future values at any later date t are unknown. It is important to note that any realization of $A_{i,t}$ translates into a balance sheet at date t, as outlined in Figure 5.3, for a single period. Ultimately, it translates into a distribution of market equity values $V_{i,t}$ at date t. Thus, asset and market values are intimately connected. Throughout, we model either asset or market equity value distributions.

The common measurement approaches are based on either tail probabilities or tail expectations of the measurement object under consideration, conditionally on a suitable event in the future. These events may be what constitutes a trigger of a systemic shock, e.g., default of a bank, macroeconomic shocks, a considerable drop in markets, political events, etc. Although our focus is on the financial system, the strengths of such shocks in modeling should be commensurate with the intention to capture systemic shocks that ultimately inflict stress on the entire economy. It appears reasonable to consider risk measures conditional on the triggers that lead to stress in the financial system since they conceptualize the risk component. However, there is also merit in unconditional measures, as they capture risks that are not clearly related to a particular trigger event, i.e., idiosyncratic risks, and thus capture general vulnerabilities of the financial system.

Although it appears obvious that the probability distribution should capture (as well as possible) the actual (future) distribution of the measurement object, the derivatives pricing literature makes a crucial distinction of this (then called objective) probability distribution to a so-called risk-neutral probability distribution. The risk-neutral probability distribution is used to price derivatives (or any contingent claim, in general) as the discounted expected future values; conversely, it can be extracted from prices of traded derivatives (contingent claims). This is an important advantage since modeling the underlying is notoriously hard, given that systemic events are fairly infrequent. The major disadvantage is that such probability measures can then be used only for pricing (other claims). For example, expected tail losses should be interpreted as the (market) premium of providing or getting insurance against systemic losses; with suitable interpretation, this provides important insights.

The risk-neutral approach is used by several authors. Merton (1974) introduces a so-called structural model that looks at the asset dynamics of individual (not necessarily financial) companies and has found applications in the credit risk literature. Lehar (2005) assumes that a multivariate continuous-time Black-Scholes model describes the asset dynamics of a portfolio of banks; he compares systemic risk of North America, Europe, and Japan and finds that larger and more profitable banks have lower systemic risk. Huang *et al.* (2009) use data on Credit-Default-Swaps to infer the probability of default and introduce a hypothetical insurance premium called the Distressed Insurance Premium. Gray and Jobst (2010) use the wedge between CDS and the credit spread implied in a structural model to assess banks' contribution to systemic risk.

5.2.3   *Data and estimation*

Systemic financial crises are rare events in developed countries, as evidenced in Figure 5.1 for the U.S. Developing economies, however, struggle with a variety of economic challenges that feed into the financial system; systemic crises are more common in these countries, see Reinhart and Rogoff (2008). Overall, however, systemic events are fairly infrequent, thus providing a challenge to estimations.

The estimation problem is compounded by the problem at hand: the goal of all measures is to say something about events in the tail of the probability distribution. Often, interest lies in estimating conditional tail events, i.e., estimating the probability of tail events conditional on other tail events. For example one may be interested in the default of one bank conditional on the distress of another bank or the system (so-called Co-Risk Measures, see Chan-Lau *et al.*, 2009b). Quantile regression methods, see Koenker (2010), aim at estimating quantiles of a dependent variable in response to changes of the independent variable in a regression type analysis. These methods have been used by Chan-Lau *et al.* (2009a) and Adrian and Brunnermeier (2016), among others.

Derivatives are claims on the tails that may allow us to infer the probability of tail events; for example, plain vanilla put options are priced taking into account the likelihood and severity of price changes below the option's exercise price, and their observed market prices may be used to extract how the market evaluates such events. Capuano (2008) introduces a framework to derive the probability of default implied by the price of equity options. Data on Credit-Default-Swaps (CDS) has been used by Tarashev and Zhu (2008), Chan-Lau *et al.* (2009a), Gray and Jobst (2010), and Giglio (2014).

While derivatives data is of good quality and is available (at good quality) for a reasonably large subset of interesting financial variables in the U.S. similar data is of good quality only for a small subset of variables in developed countries other than the U.S. and, typically, is not available at a sufficiently good quality in emerging countries. Because of our international perspective, we must refrain from such approaches and focus exclusively on either accounting or stock price data.

Extreme Value Theory (EVT), see Embrechts *et al.* (1997), studies suitable limit theorems for tail events[3] for example, they are successfully applied by Acharya *et al.* (2017) to model tail events. However, a major issue with systemic risk is joint movements. Hartmann *et al.* (2007) use multivariate extreme value theory to examine systemic risk. The literature has also studied tail correlations and modeled directly the tails and correlation therein, see, e.g., Balla *et al.* (2014). Yet, it remains a challenge to capture them accordingly. The derivatives literature has considered copulas to model such correlations. Segoviano and Goodhart (2009) introduce a so-called Banking Stability Index (BSI), which matches default probabilities

---

[3] While EVT emphasizes probabilistic regularities; Danielsson (2002) criticizes that statistical analysis performed during "normal" periods are not useful in assessing "crisis" periods.

from CDSs and reflects the expected number of banks becoming distressed given that at least one bank has become distressed. Oh and Patton (2017) study a dynamic copula model of CDS spreads to compute a joint probability of distress. Overall, most statistical approaches in the literature differ in how they strike a balance between the amount of data available (or the frequency of observations), parametric assumptions, and the tail event (how far out).

While EVT uses special techniques to estimate tail probabilities, many approaches use standard (static) econometric techniques, such as (quantile) regressions, correlation analysis, and factor analysis. Sometimes this involves common techniques in finance to deal with time-series, e.g., the SRISK approach of Brownlees and Engle (2016) assumes a GARCH model with Dynamic Conditional Correlation (DCC). We will detail this in Chapter 6 for several major techniques. For all others and a detailed discussion, see Bisias *et al.* (2012).

Market participants are concerned about losses in the market value of equity. If this is the intended application, then equity data should be the starting point of analyzing systemic risk. However, default and liquidity stress originates on the balance sheet; so if this is the intended application, then the balance sheet should be the starting point of any modeling and we are led to measure book equity and its shortfall.

Implementing balance sheet models is fraught with data difficulties: regular accounting data comes infrequently, usually quarterly at most. While using this data is conceptually appealing, infrequent reporting makes estimation difficult. To overcome the problem of infrequent data, one may make parametric assumptions about the underlying distribution of asset returns; see, e.g., Lehar (2005). Instead of parametric estimations, two solutions are proposed in the literature. The first recommends that regulators ask for more data and more observations. Along this line of reasoning, stress tests have become a regular exercise (e.g., Dodd-Frank Act Stress Tests) since the global financial crisis. In these tests, regulators request a bank to report changes to their balance sheet in response to a standardized stress event. Duffie (2014) proposes a 10-by-10-by-10 approach in which the information to be reported is significantly broadened. Also, the risk topography of Brunnermeier *et al.* (2012) suggests public reporting of sensitivities to suitably defined factors.

As an alternative to balance sheet data, the literature often looks at stock price data. Conceptually, the market value (stock price) is the residual claim on the bank's assets, so we expect both to be intimately related.

While the return on stock prices is the leveraged return on asset values, on a short frequency, say daily, the co-movement of asset returns with equity returns is approximately linear, such that statistical properties can be estimated from either book or market data. Ultimately, it may simply be a matter of convenience to use book equity or the market value of equity. For example, Hull and White (2004) propose to use equity return correlations as proxies for asset return correlations. Essentially, it is an empirical issue if we can infer the statistical properties of assets sufficiently well from stock prices. There is hope. Duellmann *et al.* (2010) argue that correlation estimates from equity returns are more efficient than those from default rates. Moreover, several authors use stock market data in a balance sheet framework; e.g., Brownlees and Engle (2016) use this to calculate capital shortfall and their SRISK measure.

5.3 An overview of measures based on market data

Systemic risk has many dimensions. Bisias *et al.* (2012) study them from various angles in four tables that dissect risk measures by their data requirements, by their supervisory scope, by their event/decision time horizon, and finally by their research method. Table 5.1 characterizes popular systemic risk measures in the literature based on market data, with a particular focus on application and the associated tradeoffs of a modeler. A full description of all these measure is beyond the scope of this table; consequently, we describe in detail the main measures only, in the next chapter. For other measures, see Bisias *et al.* (2012) and Upper (2011); for a comparison, see Benoit *et al.* (2013).

Table 5.1: Overview of risk measures based on market data.

Authors	Reference	Description	Data Requirements, Approach & Estimation
		Panel A: Based on returns	
Adrian and Brunnermeier (2016)	ΔCoVaR	Change in VaR of system conditional on stress of a bank, a bank conditional on system stress	Weekly equity returns (balance sheet and state variables' data for conditional version); quantile regression
BCBS (2014)	Bank score	Weighted average of 12 scores; score for each variable derived as banks' values divided by sample total; sample totals derived from 75 banks, published by BCBS	12 indicators across five categories (total and intra-financial system exposures, notional amounts of certain assets, cross-country exposures)
Acharya *et al.* (2017)	MES	Expected loss of a bank when the market falls below a threshold (often q-VaR)	Daily equity returns, S&P 500 market returns, $q = 5\%$; calculated as average bank return on days when market drops by at least 5%

Brownlees and Engle (2016)	SRISK	Capital shortfall of a bank based on long-run MES; long-run MES characterized through time-varying conditional volatility and correlation (GARCH-DCC)	Equity returns and balance sheet data; (quasi-) maximum likelihood for estimation and simulation using residuals
Kritzman et al. (2011)	Absorption Ratio (AR)	Fraction of (total) variance explained by a fixed number of factors	Daily returns for 51 industries; Principal Component Analysis (PCA) using 500-day rolling windows
Billio et al. (2012)	Systemic contribution (PCAS) & Granger causality networks	PCAS: exposure of a bank to movements in a number of factors that explain a threshold fraction; number of Granger causal relationships to total possible causal relationships	36-month rolling windows of monthly returns (banks, insurers, brokers, hedge funds)
Kreis and Leisen (2018)	Single factor loadings & ΔCEDF	Size of loadings in a single factor model as a measure of interconnectedness; difference in expected conditional default frequency with/without interconnections	Daily equity returns for the 15 largest banks; monthly exploratory factor analysis on rolling 3-month windows

(Continued)

Table 5.1: (*Continued*)

		Panel B: Based on Credit Default Swaps (CDS)	
Huang *et al.* (2009)	Distressed Insurance Premium (DIP)	Price of insurance against systemic financial stress	High-frequency equity returns and weekly CDS data; banking system model analogous portfolio credit risk models; risk-neutral probability of default from CDS; asset return correlation from equity return correlation, past correlations, and explanatory variables; risk-neutral simulations to determine price of insurance
Giglio (2014)	Joint default probability	Probability bounds on systemic events	Joint default risk of pairs of banks from CDS spreads, taking account of counterparty risk; individual default risk from bond prices
Chan-Lau *et al.* (2009a)	Co-Risk	Change in VaR conditional on quantile of joint default probability	CDS rates; implied default probabilities; quantile regression

Panel C: Tail estimations

Hartmann *et al.* (2007)	Contagion risk and tail-β	Measuring extreme spillovers among banks and the exposure of banks to extreme systematic shocks	Multivariate extreme value estimators based on daily equity prices of European and U.S. banks
Balla *et al.* (2014)	Tail dependence	Asymptotic dependence rate	Multivariate extreme value estimators based daily stock returns of 29 U.S. deposit institutions
Segoviano and Goodhart (2009)	Banking stability index (BSI)	Joint probability of default	Daily CDS rates; multivariate density estimation via entropy maximization subject to default probability constraints
Hautsch *et al.* (2015)	Realized systemic risk beta	Marginal effect of a firm's Value-at-risk (VaR) on the system's VaR	57 U.S. financial institutions; daily equity prices, quarterly balance sheet data, and 7 state variables; LASSO type regressions
Capuano (2008)	Implied Probability of Default (iPoD)	Individual default probabilities	Daily stock and option price data of the ten largest U.S. banks; cross-entropy minimization subject to balance sheet and option pricing constraints

(Continued)

Table 5.1: (*Continued*)

Gray and Jobst (2010)	Systemic CCA	Measure of governments' implicit guarantees	Daily equity prices, daily CDS spreads and quarterly balance sheet data; for a portfolio of banks, first estimate each bank's expected loss using contingent claims analysis, then determine system expected shortfall using copulas (generalized extreme value distributions)
Giesecke and Kim (2011)	Default intensity model (DIM)	Number of economy-wide defaults over a fixed time in the future	Data on all corporate defaults 1970–2008; regime-switching, reduced-form continuous-time model for timing of bank defaults in the system
Lehar (2005)	Expected shortfall	Expected future liability of regulator	Banking system model analogous portfolio credit risk models; applied to North American, European, and Japanese banking systems; monthly equity prices and annual balance sheet data; estimation of an exponentially weighted moving average of covariances

Chapter 6

Main systemic risk measures

Classical measures to assess market risk are Value-at-Risk (VaR) and Expected Shortfall (ES). In addition, factor models have been very popular to assess the credit risk of banks; see Crosbie and Bohn (2002) and Saunders and Cornett (2009).

These major risk measurement approaches are also at the root of major approaches to measure systemic risk. The following three sections describe measures based on Value-at-Risk, those based on expected shortfall, and those based on factor models. The chapter ends with a fourth section that compares the different approaches.

All measures presented in this chapter are based on stock returns R_i ($i = 1, \ldots, N$) and the market return

$$R_m = \sum_{i=1}^{N} \omega_i R_i, \tag{6.1}$$

where ω_i is the weight of bank i.

6.1 Measures based on Value-at-Risk

Value-at-Risk is defined with reference to a return R with a continuous distribution over a given time horizon, and a given (large) probability q. It is the q-quantile of the (return) loss $L = 1 - R$, i.e.,

$$P[L \leq VaR^q] = q. \tag{6.2}$$

In other words, it is the threshold loss with the property that q is the probability of the event that the loss is less than that threshold. (Throughout this section, for simplicity of exposition, we study the loss based on the net return $1 - R$. Alternatively, the loss is often defined as $L = E[R] - R$, which can be studied analogously.) In practice, common values are $q = 99\%$

over a two-week horizon in the market risk literature and $q = 99.9\%$ over a one-year horizon in the credit-risk literature.

Hautsch *et al.* (2015) study the total time-varying marginal effect of a firm's Value-at-Risk on the system's VaR and provide statistical evidence that it captures companies' systemic importance in the U.S. financial system. Allen *et al.* (2012b) derive an aggregate systemic risk measure (CATFIN) using the 99%-VaR based on cross-sectional returns of financial institutions; they document that it forecasts economic downturns almost one year ahead. Cai *et al.* (2018) introduce a measure of interconnectedness; they document a positive correlation between their measure and several systemic risk measures that mainly arises during recessions. Moreover, they find that interconnectedness increases aggregate systemic risk (CATFIN) in recessions.

Adrian and Brunnermeier (2016) introduce Conditional Value-at-Risk (CoVaR), which is the VaR for a suitable *conditional* probability distribution. To be precise, we denote the conditioning by C, which can be either a random variable or a measurable set, such that the conditional probability distribution reads $P[\cdot|C]$. With reference to a (return) L with continuous distribution, the CoVaR is defined analogous to Equation (6.2) as

$$P[L \leq \mathrm{CoVaR}^{C,q}|C] = q. \tag{6.3}$$

The idea of Adrian and Brunnermeier (2016) is to study this in relation to two events that both relate to the (return) loss $\tilde{L}$ of another random variable $\tilde{R}$. First, they define the stress event as the event that the random variable $\tilde{L}$ is *exactly* at its q-VaR, i.e., $C = \{\tilde{L} = q - \mathrm{VaR}\}$; and, second, they define the normal event as the event that the random variable $\tilde{L}$ is *exactly* at the median state, i.e., $C = \{\tilde{L} = 0.5 - \mathrm{VaR}\}$. (Girardi and Ergun (2013) extend this and change the definition of financial distress from an institution being exactly at its VaR to being at most at its VaR.) To measure systemic risk, Adrian and Brunnermeier (2016) then study

$$\Delta\mathrm{CoVaR} = \mathrm{CoVaR}^{\mathrm{stress},q} - \mathrm{CoVaR}^{\mathrm{normal},q}.$$

This difference between two CoVaR values reflects the pure systemic contribution. The first of these values is conditional on a suitably defined stress event, and the other is conditional on a normal period.

For an individual bank $i = 1, \dots, N$, Adrian and Brunnermeier (2016) study $\Delta\mathrm{CoVaR}$ using $R = R_m$ and $\tilde{R} = R_i$, i.e, $L_m = 1 - R_m$ and $\tilde{L}_i = 1 - R_i$. In other words, $\Delta\mathrm{CoVaR}$ is defined as the change in VaR of the market return (financial system) conditional on bank i being under distress (at its q-VaR) relative to being at its median state (at its 0.5-VaR).

Adrian and Brunnermeier (2016) stress that ΔCoVaR is directional, i.e., switching $R, \tilde{R}$ usually changes its value and that this switching radically changes the interpretation. They also define the so-called Exposure-ΔCoVaR, which is the CoVaR concept applied using $R = R_i$ and $\tilde{R} = R_m$ and reveals the bank's increase in VaR in the event of a financial crisis.

To get a description of the risk of the entire financial system, one may then want to aggregate the individual ΔCoVaR$_i$ of banks $i = 1, \ldots, N$ to a systemic risk measure. The measure ΔCoVaR$_i$ of Adrian and Brunnermeier (2016) characterizes the contribution of individual banks to the risk of the financial system, whereas their Exposure-ΔCoVaR$_i$ characterizes the contribution of the market to the risk of individual bank i. This leads us to base the aggregated system ΔCoVaR on Exposure-ΔCoVaR, i.e., we define

$$\Delta\text{CoVaR}_{system} = \sum_{i=1}^{N} \omega_i \cdot \text{Exposure-}\Delta\text{CoVaR}_i. \qquad (6.4)$$

Adrian and Brunnermeier (2016) advocate quantile regression to estimate ΔCoVaR. We apply it here to their Exposure-ΔCoVaR. Unconditional quantile regression of the financial system's losses on losses of an individual bank i for the q-quantile are, then,

$$\hat{R}_i = \hat{\alpha}_{q,i} + \hat{\beta}_{q,i} R_m,$$

where $\hat{R}_i$ is the predicted value for the q-quantile loss of bank i, conditional on loss realization R_m of the financial system. Then, analogous to Equation (10) in Adrian and Brunnermeier (2016),

$$\text{Exposure-}\Delta\text{CoVaR}_i = \hat{\beta}_{q,i}(\text{VaR}^q - \text{VaR}^{0.5}),$$

where $\text{VaR}^q, \text{VaR}^{0.5}$ denote the q-VaR and 0.5-VaR based on the market return R_m.

The unconditional quantile regression presented so far assumes that ΔCoVaR is constant over time; in addition, Adrian and Brunnermeier (2016) present a conditional version that estimates ΔCoVaR over time, conditional on suitable state variables.

6.2 Measures based on expected shortfall

6.2.1 *Systemic and marginal expected shortfall*

For a given threshold c, return distribution R, and associated (return) loss $L = 1 - R$, expected shortfall is the expected loss for the distribution that is conditional on losses exceeding c, i.e.,

$$\text{ES} = E[L|L \geq c].$$

Acharya *et al.* (2017) apply this to the market return R_m defined in Equation (6.1). They derive from there the sensitivity to bank i,

$$\text{MES}_i = \frac{\partial \text{ES}}{\partial \omega_i} = E[L_i|L_m \geq c],$$

which they refer to as marginal expected shortfall (MES). Herein, c describes the bank's expected (relative) equity loss when the market (return) falls below a threshold c. They interpret this as the systemic event, i.e., the stress event. Often, c is taken as the q-VaR, the Value-at-Risk for the market return R_m at a given probability q.

The value MES_i characterizes the (marginal) contribution of individual banks to the risk of the financial system. To get a description of the risk of the entire financial system, we aggregate the so-determined individual MES_i of banks $i = 1, \ldots, N$ to a systemic risk measure

$$\text{MES}_{system} = \sum_{i=1}^{N} \omega_i \cdot \text{MES}_i = E[L_m|L_m \geq c]. \tag{6.5}$$

Acharya *et al.* (2017) further introduce a theoretical model in which the systemic component of an individual bank i is driven by externalities of financial crises. They assume that banks have to hold a fraction k of assets as equity and this leads them to study systemic expected shortfall SES_i, defined as the expected capital shortfall of bank i conditional on a crisis C, i.e.,

$$SES_i = E\left[kA_{i,s} - E_{i,s+1} \middle| \sum_{i=1}^{N} E_{i,s+1} < k \sum_{i=1}^{N} A_{i,s}\right].$$

Here, the crisis is characterized by the situation where *total* equity of all banks is below k times *total* assets. Therein, k is the prudential capital fraction, usually set at 8%. It is important to note that this describes the absolute "loss" (monetary value), whereas MES_i describes a relative loss.

Acharya *et al.* (2017) study daily returns, set $q = 95\%$ and use "large" drops in the market return as crisis events. They use either the S&P 500 as the market return (see the legend in their Table 1) or the value-weighted market return provided by CRSP (see the legend in their Table 3). Overall, they suggest estimating MES_i non-parametrically as the average bank return R_i on days when the market drops by at least the 95%-VaR.

Estimation of SES is hard, so Acharya *et al.* (2017) postulate a two-factor model (see Section 6.3) with power law distributions. The use of power law distributions is motivated by Extreme Value Theory, which argues that they capture well the tail, which is the focus of systemic risk measurement. Then, Acharya *et al.* (2017) use properties of the power law distribution to express

$$\text{SES}_i = (kL_{is} - 1 + \theta\text{MES}_i + \Delta_i)E_{i,s},$$

where $L_{i,s} = A_{i,s}/E_{i,s}$ describes the leverage and θ, Δ_i are constants. While Δ_i is characterized mathematically, unfortunately, it is not straightforward to implement. Acharya *et al.* (2017) argue that SES is driven by leverage and MES, and find empirical support for this. They also demonstrate empirically that its components would have helped in predicting systemic risk during the GFC.

6.2.2 *SRISK*

While SES is an appealing concept, it suffers from three major drawbacks that SRISK addresses. First, the time horizon is daily, but one would like to measure systemic risk at longer time horizons. Second, the intended application would benefit from a dynamic (conditional) parametric modeling that better helps to predict the build-up of systemic risks. Third, the empirical implementation is made hard by the Δ_i term, which boils down to conditioning on the crisis event.

To address the first issue, Brownlees and Engle (2016) consider a time horizon of six months and refer to the associated marginal expected shortfall over this horizon as *Long Run Marginal Expected Shortfall (LRMES)*. Analogous to MES, it characterizes the relative drop in the market value of equity over the respective time horizon, conditional on a crisis (a significant drop in the broad market). Acharya *et al.* (2012) note that one may approximate this as $\text{LRMES} \approx 1 - \exp(-18 \cdot \text{MES})$ using the 1-day MES based on the concept of crisis characterized as market losses larger than -2%.

Building upon the concept of capital shortfall inherent in the concept of systemic risk, Acharya *et al.* (2012) introduce SRISK as the expected capital shortfall conditional on being in a crisis. For a bank $i = 1, \ldots, N$, the capital shortfall at date $s+1$ can be expressed as $kD_{i,s+1} - (1-k)E_{i,s+1}$ using the prudential capital fraction k (analogous to SES). Since capital shortfall is based on book values, while LRMES is based on market values, they conjecture that the book value of debt will be mostly unchanged and that the drop in equity is well approximated by its LRMES. Overall, this gives for bank $i = 1, \ldots, N$ the expected capital shortfall as

$$\text{SRISK}_i = kD_i - (1-k)E_i(1 - \text{LRMES}_i),$$

see Equation (1) in Brownlees and Engle (2016). Note that SRISK is a function of the size of the firm, its degree of leverage, and its expected equity loss conditional on the market decline (LRMES).

The LRMES$_i$ is determined by the (conditional) joint distribution of (R_i, R_m); Brownlees and Engle (2016) assume that this joint distribution is characterized by time varying volatility for σ_i and σ_m according to the GJR-GARCH (Glosten *et al.*, 1993) and time-varying conditional correlation according to the GARCH-DCC, see Engle (2009) for details. The dynamic component is a crucial part of the model that addresses the second drawback of SES that we mentioned above: in theory, such a dynamic process should be able to reflect better the future build-up of systemic risk. (This addresses the criticism of Danielsson, 2002, that models in "normal" periods are not good at predicting "crisis" periods.)

There are well-established conditional estimation approaches for the GJR-GARCH/GARCH-DCC processes underlying (R_i, R_m), see Engle (2009). While there are no closed-form expressions for LRMES, this value can be calculated well through so-called Monte-Carlo simulation approaches. Brownlees and Engle (2016) recommend using standardized residuals of the GARCH-DCC calibration exercise to prevent imposing parametric restrictions on the innovations.

The so-calculated SRISK$_i$ characterizes the capital shortfall of a bank $i = 1, \ldots, N$ in the system when the system is in a crisis. To get the capital shortfall SRISK of the entire financial system, Brownlees and Engle (2016) sum up the non-negative shortfall of all banks in the system:

$$\text{SRISK}_{system} = \sum_{i=1}^{N} \max\left\{\text{SRISK}_i, 0\right\}. \tag{6.6}$$

6.3   Measures based on factor models

Factor models aim at describing the set of returns $(R_i)_{i=1,\ldots,N}$ through a set of common random variables, called factors. Specifically, they assume that the relative changes are driven by changes in factors, say, with K factors:

$$R_i = a_{i0} + \sum_{j=1}^{K} a_{ij} \cdot Y_j + \varepsilon_i, \tag{6.7}$$

for all banks $i = 1, \ldots, N$. Here, $(Y_j)_{j=1,\ldots,K}$ are the so-called factors. They are random variables that are assumed to be independent of each other and of the random variables ε_i. The parameters a_{ij} are constants that describe the individual *loading* on (a.k.a. sensitivity to) factor $j = 1, \ldots, K$.

Equation (6.7) introduces time-independent factor models. They correspond to unconditional factor models, but they may be defined analogously in a conditional way. Chapter 7 presents estimates over rolling time windows, with changing loadings over time; this corresponds to a form of time-dependent factor models.

Typically, banks are linked across a variety of dimensions; they may be interconnected via the interbank market, via investments in similar assets, or in many other different ways. In structural models this boils down to co-movement in the factors. From an econometrician's viewpoint, this parametrizes the estimation problem, and we use appropriate estimation techniques with given factors or carry out principal component analysis (PCA) in case we do not want to impose specific factors.

It is common to work with so-called scores (standardized returns), i.e., define for banks $i = 1, \ldots, N$:

$$\mu_i = E[R_i], \quad \sigma_i^2 = Var(R_i), \quad V_i = \frac{R_i - \mu_i}{\sigma_i}.$$

Then, the starting point of the modeler is no longer Equation (6.7), but

$$V_i = \sum_{j=1}^{K} a_{ij} \cdot Y_j + \varepsilon_i, \tag{6.8}$$

for all banks $i = 1, \ldots, N$. Therein, V_i $(i = 1, \ldots, N)$ are random variables with zero expectation and unit variance. As before, the random variables $(Y_j)_{j=1,\ldots,K}$ are assumed to be independent of each other and of the random variables ε_i.

6.3.1 *Principal component analysis*

Principal component analysis (PCA) is a common technique in finance for finding uncorrelated factor(s) that best explain a cross-section of data. From a statistical perspective, the PCA is a variable reduction technique. It aims at reducing a larger set of variables into a smaller set of (artificial) factors. Observations of correlated variables are converted into values of uncorrelated variables via orthogonal linear transformation. These uncorrelated variables are called the principal components; usually a small number of them accounts for most of the variance in observations, see, e.g., Jolliffe (2002) and Muirhead (2005). It is common to sort them in decreasing importance in explaining (residual) variance.

When PCA is applied to the financial system, there are periods when a smaller (larger) number of factors explain some fraction of the (variance of the) data; the number of factors are taken as an indicator that the interconnectedness has decreased (increased).

In Kritzman *et al.* (2011) and Billio *et al.* (2012), the system's aggregate return is defined as $R_S = \sum_{i=1}^{N} R_i$. Volatilities are denoted as $\sigma_i^2 = Var(R_i)$ and $\sigma_S^2 = Var(R_S)$ for the system. Mathematically, at most N factors are necessary to explain the (observed) returns of the N banks in our financial system. Kritzman *et al.* (2011) and Billio *et al.* (2012) define the risk (variance) explained through the first $1 \leq n \leq N$ factors as

$$\omega_n = \sum_{j=1}^{n} Var(Y_j)$$

and study the ratio of the explained to the total variance ω_n/ω_N. For a given number of factors n, Kritzman *et al.* (2011) study the so-called Absorption Ratio (AR), defined as

$$\text{AR} = \frac{\omega_n}{\omega_N},$$

the fraction of the total return variance explained ("absorbed") by the given fixed number of factors n. (They set n to be approximately equal to a fifth of the total number of banks N.) A high (low) value corresponds to a high (low) level of systemic risk because it implies the sources of risk are more unified (disparate). Kritzman *et al.* (2011) use daily returns for the 51 industries of the MSCI U.S. index from January 1, 1998 to January 31, 2010. They carry out the PCA using 500-day windows and fix the number of eigenvectors at approximately one-fifth the number of assets. They find that the most significant U.S. stock market draw-downs followed spikes in (changes of) the AR.

For a given number of factors, Billio *et al.* (2012) are interested in the time periods when the absorption ratio exceeds a given threshold H:

$$\frac{\omega_n}{\omega_N} \geq H.$$

They use this to detect time periods of increased linkage and similarities in risk exposures.

The contribution of institution i to the risk of the system is then defined as

$$\mathrm{PCAS}_{i,n} = \frac{1}{2} \frac{\sigma_i^2}{\sigma_S^2} \frac{\partial \sigma_S^2}{\partial \sigma_i^2}\bigg|_{h_n \geq H} = \frac{1}{\sigma_S^2} \sum_{k=1}^{n} \sigma_i^2 a_{ik} Var(Y_k)\bigg|_{h_n \geq H},$$

conditional on a strong common component across banks ($h_n \geq H$).

This corresponds to the exposure of bank i to the total risk of the system, measured as the weighted average of the square of the factor loadings of the single bank i to the first n principal components, where the weights are factor variances. Billio et al. (2012) study co-movements in the U.S. financial sector, consisting of banks, brokers, insurers, and hedge funds. They estimate this on rolling windows of 36-months, and track the relative magnitudes of the first factors. They find that the first and second principal components capture the majority of return variation from 1994–2008.

6.3.2 The size and heterogeneity of single factor loadings

Kreis and Leisen (2018) assume a single factor model based on Equation (6.8), i.e.,

$$V_{it} = a_{it} \cdot Y_t + \sqrt{1 - a_{it}^2} \cdot \varepsilon_{it}. \tag{6.9}$$

Here the random variables Y, ε_i, $i = 1, \ldots, N$ are (serially) independent with zero expectation and unit variance.

The single factor framework means that for any pair of banks $i, j = 1, \ldots, N$:

$$Correl(V_i, V_j) = Cov(V_i, V_j) = a_i a_j Var(Y) = a_i a_j$$

describes the correlation of risk-adjusted asset values for any combination of individual banks i, j. In this regard, loadings are closely related to correlations.

A single factor model captures some important aspects of systemic risk through loadings (correlations). For example, Elsinger et al. (2006) assess financial stability of a network model of Austrian interbank loans and find that correlation in banks' asset portfolios dominates contagion as the main source of systemic risk. Also, the propagation effects of Acemoglu et al. (2015) suggest that the initial idiosyncratic shock boils down to a systematic shock affecting a (very) large number of banks over some time period.

The loading a_i is a characterization of the joint movement of V_i (individual banks) with the factor (the financial system) and, thereby, characterizes a form of interconnectedness. To get a description of the interconnectedness across the entire financial system, one may then want to aggregate this to the average loading

$$a_{system} = \sum_{i=1}^{N} \frac{a_i}{N}. \qquad (6.10)$$

The model of Kreis and Leisen (2018) is rooted in structural models used in the credit risk literature and, therefore, they are interested in asset returns. Due to data limitations, they do use equity returns to estimate the loadings via factor analysis, a form of PCA. Their estimation uses daily data for the 15 largest banks in the U.S. over the course 1980–2016 to estimate the conditional loadings using rolling windows of 3 months. They find that average loadings have considerably increased and the heterogeneity in loadings across banks has decreased over time, and they identify four major regimes.

From a conceptual perspective, Kreis and Leisen (2018) differ from the PCA analysis through the focus on a *single* component and the underlying (model) assumptions of a factor analysis versus a principal component analysis (PCA). From a purely mathematical perspective, this is akin to the difference between analyzing eigenvalues of a PCA (Kritzman *et al.*, 2011; Billio *et al.*, 2012) and analyzing its eigenvectors (Kreis and Leisen, 2018).

The temporal evolution of (average) loadings and their heterogeneity provides interesting insights into interconnectedness across time. Thus, loadings give additional insights into an important aspect of systemic risk.

6.3.3   *Conditional expected default frequency*

Kreis and Leisen (2018) study the single factor model of the previous section in the spirit of structural models from the credit risk literature. They assume that each bank in the system may default on its obligations to derive a systemic risk measure that characterizes the aggregate default in the financial system.

This measure refers to a balance sheet notion of default discussed in section 5.2.1. To explain the default notion in greater detail, we refer to the notation introduced there and fix a date s and a bank $i = 1, \ldots, N$. Kreis and Leisen (2018) assume that default occurs over the time period between dates s and $s + 1$ when equity is reduced below a critical threshold, e.g., $A_{i,s+1} < D_{i,s+1}$. This approach takes a stylized view on default that is common in the structural model literature on companies (non-financials).[1]

For banks $i = 1, \ldots, N$ and dates s, they define a threshold parameter $K_{i,s}$ based on debt and asset values that characterizes default: bank $i = 1, \ldots, N$ defaults when $V_i < K_i$. They further define

$$p_i = P[V_i < K_i], \quad \bar{p} = \frac{1}{N} \sum_{i=1}^{N} p_i \tag{6.11}$$

and note that p_i describes the (individual) default probability of bank $i = 1, \ldots, N$ and that $\bar{p}$ captures the average default probability. While the threshold parameter $K_{i,s}$ is rooted in the balance sheet, structural models treat it as a parameter to be calibrated; Kreis and Leisen (2018) set it such that default probability p_i of a bank i is at a preset target level.

The expectation of the default frequency M_N introduced above fulfills

$$E[M_N] = \frac{1}{N} \sum_{i=1}^{N} E[X_i] = \bar{p}. \tag{6.12}$$

For an informative measure of risk in the banking system, Kreis and Leisen (2018) are interested in the departures of M_N from its expectation; they focus on those default frequencies M_N that *exceed* the expectation. For that purpose, they define a measure of risk in the entire banking system, called the *Conditional Expected Default Frequency (CEDF)* by setting

$$\text{CEDF}(a, N) = E\left[M_N \,|\, M_N \geq E[M_N]\right].$$

This depends on (the vector of) all banks' loadings $a = (a_i)_{i=1,\ldots,N}$, on the number of banks N and (although not referenced explicitly) on the individual default probabilities $p_i, i = 1, \ldots, N$.

Loadings characterize banks' interconnectedness. To measure the systemic risk of interconnected banks, Kreis and Leisen (2018) are interested in the risk in the banking system stemming from linkages in excess of the risk in a banking system without linkages $(a_i = 0; i = 1, \ldots, N)$. For this, they introduce

$$\Delta\text{CEDF}(a, N) = \text{CEDF}(a, N) - \text{CEDF}(0, N).$$

For implementation they study a time period of one year and assume that the random variables Y, ε_i $(i = 1, \ldots, N)$ are standard normal, such that the individual default probability in Equation (6.11) can be calculated

---

[1] An important aspect of regulation is the requirement that banks hold sufficient equity, i.e., the requirement that equity is larger than some strictly positive value. This could be studied analogously through a judicious re-interpretation of debt.

as $p_i = P[V_i < K_i] = \mathcal{N}(K_i)$, where $\mathcal{N}$ denotes the cumulative distribution function for standard normal random variables and by $\mathcal{N}^{-1}$ its inverse.

Kreis and Leisen (2018) document that the ΔCEDF systemic risk measure increases non-linearly both in the average loading of banks and in the homogeneity of banks' loadings (measured through the difference between maximum and minimum loadings). Coupled with their empirical analysis of loadings, their measure shows that systemic risk became critical in the last of their four regimes, i.e., over the most recent time period from May 2007 to September 2016.

6.4   Comparison

For a theoretical comparison of the measures presented in the previous section, we assume that the (conditional) joint distribution of the stock return R_i for a bank $i = 1, \ldots, N$ and of the market return R_m are bivariate normal with zero expectation, and denote by σ_i, σ_m their standard deviations as well as by ρ_{im} their correlation. Under this assumption, Acharya *et al.* (2012) find, see their Equations (12, 13), that

$$\Delta\text{CoVaR}_i = \rho_{im}\sigma_m\mathcal{N}^{-1}(q), \text{ and} \qquad (6.13)$$

$$\text{MES}_i = \sigma_i\rho_{im}E\left[\frac{L_m}{\sigma_m}\bigg|\frac{L_m}{\sigma_m} \geq \frac{c}{\sigma_m}\right], \qquad (6.14)$$

where q and c correspond to the quantiles that underlie the characterization of the stress event within their respective methodologies, and $\mathcal{N}^{-1}$ describes the inverse of the cumulative standard normal distribution function. Löffler and Raupach (2018) provide an explicit derivation of both terms, see their Equations (3, 7). In addition, their Equation (6) shows that

$$\text{Exposure-}\Delta\text{CoVaR}_i = \rho_{im}\sigma_i\mathcal{N}^{-1}(q). \qquad (6.15)$$

Brownlees and Engle (2016) report that LRMES_i can be approximated by

$$\text{LRMES}_i = -\sqrt{h}\sigma_i\rho_{im}\frac{\varphi(c/\sigma_m)}{\mathcal{N}(c/\sigma_m)},$$

where φ denotes the density of a standard normal and h measures the length of the time horizon. Under this assumption, we then have

$$\text{SRISK}_i = kD_i - (1-k)E_i\left(1 - \sqrt{h}\sigma_i\rho_{i,m}\frac{\varphi(c/\sigma_m)}{\mathcal{N}(c/\sigma_m)}\right). \qquad (6.16)$$

Hence, SRISK_i would be mostly driven by k, the prudential capital fraction, by debt, equity, and idiosyncratic volatility as well as correlation. However, given that their modeling relies on GJR-GARCH/GARCH-DCC processes, the stated approximation of $LRMES_i$ may well deteriorate in some circumstances. We return to this briefly at the end of Chapter 7, when we discuss the main insights of that chapter.

In a Gaussian framework, Billio *et al.* (2012) show in their online appendix that their PCAS measure is related to the contribution of the i-th institution to the multivariate tail dynamics of the system.

Brownlees *et al.* (2015) find ΔCoVaR and SRISK to be useful in alerting of historical bank runs between January 1866 and December 1925. However, Zhang *et al.* (2015) question empirically whether purely stock-based measures capture systemic risk adequately. Moreover, Löffler and Raupach (2018) identify non-exotic cases in which a change in a bank's systematic risk, idiosyncratic risk, size, or contagiousness increase the risk of the system but lower its measured systemic risk contributions. Similarly, Benoit *et al.* (2017) use regulatory data for 119 U.S. and international banks, and document that the current scoring methodology severely distorts the allocation of regulatory capital among banks. Benoit *et al.* (2013) provide an empirical comparison of systemic risk measures.

Kupiec and Guntay (2016) criticize empirically that current risk measures essentially measure systematic risk instead of systemic risk. To see at a theoretical level where this is rooted, let us assume again normal distributed returns. Then, in Equations (6.13, 6.14, 6.15) the terms $\mathcal{N}^{-1}(q)$ and $E\left[\frac{L_m}{\sigma_m}\middle|\frac{L_m}{\sigma_m} \geq \frac{c}{\sigma_m}\right]$ are both constants. This suggests that the ΔCoVaR$_i$, Exposure-ΔCoVaR$_i$, and the MES$_i$ systemic risk measures are driven linearly by correlation, which is closely related to the market beta measure of systematic risk. In addition, $\varphi(c/\sigma_m)$ is a constant such that equation (6.16) suggests that SRISK is driven linearly by correlation. This theoretical analysis on ΔCoVaR$_i$, Exposure-ΔCoVaR$_i$, MES$_i$ and SRISK$_i$ support the empirical observation of Kupiec and Guntay (2016).

The three measures, Exposure-ΔCoVaR$_i$, MES$_i$ and SRISK$_i$, assess the systemic risk of an individual bank in the system. Although neither Adrian and Brunnermeier (2016) nor Acharya *et al.* (2017) aggregate their individual measures to get a measure of systemic risk in the entire system, we find it useful to do so. Therefore, we aggregate them through a weighted average to get the two measures ΔCoVaR$_{system}$, MES$_{system}$ of systemic risk for the entire financial system, see Equations (6.4, 6.5). We can write under the normality assumption and the notation leading to Equations (6.14, 6.15):

$$\Delta\text{CoVaR}_{system} = \left(\sum_{i=1}^{N} \omega_i \rho_{im} \sigma_i\right) \mathcal{N}^{-1}(q) = \sigma_m \mathcal{N}^{-1}(q),$$

$$\text{MES}_{system} = \left(\sum_{i=1}^{N} \omega_i \rho_{im} \sigma_i\right) E\left[R_m \,|\, R_m < c\right] = \sigma_m E\left[R_m \,|\, R_m < c\right].$$

Based on the formula for expected shortfall of a standard normal distribution, we find for $q = c = 99\%$ that $\mathcal{N}^{-1}(q) = 2.326$ and $E\left[R_m \,|\, R_m < c\right] = 2.665$, so that we have $\Delta\text{CoVaR}_{system} < \text{MES}_{system}$.

The loadings of Kreis and Leisen (2018) are closely related to correlation but provide an additional (conceptionally simple) view on interconnectedness that has been ignored so far.

The ΔCEDF measure is defined at the level of the entire financial system. While the ΔCEDF measure of Kreis and Leisen (2018) builds upon loadings, the dependence is non-linear; an increase in average loadings and a decrease in heterogeneity both lead to an increase in the ΔCEDF measure.

Chapter 7

Systemic risk around the world

This chapter studies the temporal evolution of systemic risk from 2000 to 2016. We use a dataset consisting of 578 banks and covering the geographical regions of the world that we looked at in Chapter 1.

Our main goal is to provide an overview of systemic risk worldwide. In addition, we want to compare the major systemic risk measures presented in Chapter 5 and identify empirical similarities and differences. We describe the dataset and implementation in the first section; in the following three sections, we look at systemic risk worldwide, across six world regions, and country by country. We summarize our main insights in the fourth section.

7.1 Dataset and implementation issues

Our dataset covers 578 banks in 51 countries that make up a major index of worldwide banks in March 2017. Table 7.1 describes the countries and the number of their banks covered. Notably, the largest and second largest number of banks are from the U.S. and Japan, respectively. In general, our sample covers roughly a single digit number of banks in each country in our sample.

For each bank in the dataset, we have daily data on the total return, adjusted for dividend payments, stock splits, etc. To aid comparisons, the total return of each bank on any given day is converted to U.S. dollars using the current exchange rate. We then calculate daily net returns that are the major input to our estimation of systemic risk. Throughout, we implement the main systemic risk measures presented in Chapter 5 for the system: MES, ΔCoVaR, SRISK, loadings, and ΔCEDF.

The ΔCoVaR and MES methods require the definition of a market return. In line with Equation (6.1), we define it as the return on the portfolio

Table 7.1: The number of banks in each country that are covered in the dataset.

Country	Number of Banks	Country	Number of Banks	Country	Number of Banks
Abu Dhabi	5	Greece	5	Philippines	10
Argentina	6	HK	8	Poland	11
Australia	8	Hungary	1	Portugal	2
Austria	2	India	35	Qatar	9
Bahrain	8	Indonesia	14	Russia	2
Belgium	2	Ireland	2	Singapore	3
Brazil	9	Israel	6	S. Africa	6
Canada	11	Italy	15	S. Korea	9
Chile	6	Japan	72	Spain	8
China	14	Kuwait	11	Sweden	9
Czech Rep.	2	Malaysia	10	Switzerland	6
Denmark	5	Mexico	6	Taiwan	16
Dubai	2	Morocco	4	Thailand	10
Egypt	3	Netherl.	2	Turkey	10
Finland	1	Norway	5	UK	12
France	3	Oman	8	USA	146
Germany	4	Pakistan	12	Vietnam	4

consisting of all the banks under consideration, i.e., the market return is the average bank return of that portfolio using capitalization weights. The total capitalization of the banks in our data set is dominated by some banks in our sample that are significantly larger than others. While this is not an issue for ΔCoVaR, MES, SRISK, and loadings, ΔCEDF assumes (implicitly) that all banks are approximately of similar size. Therefore, for ΔCEDF we restrict ourselves, separately at each month, to the banks that have market capitalization not less than the 95 percentile, leaving us in the worldwide analysis of ΔCEDF with a total of 41 banks covered at different times over the time period 2000–2016. For our regional analysis, our ΔCEDF analysis reduces the banks in the North American, European, Asian, and Africa/Middle East to a maximum of 30, 19, and 19 banks, respectively; in Latin America and Australia, we study all the banks in our sample.

Not all the banks traded from 2000 and not all continue trading to the end 2016; we add (delete) them from our analysis as the data (no longer) permits us. For this, we clean the data, on a monthly (rolling) basis, in two ways. First, we drop days for which less than one-half of the banks have return data; second, we drop banks for which more than 10% of the daily return data over the previous 12-month time window are missing. This cleaning means that the analysis is on a different number of banks at different times.

There are slight differences in the implementation of the original methods. While Adrian and Brunnermeier (2016) use weekly data and implement ΔCoVaR conditional on a variety of state variables, we implement it using daily data over rolling windows of 12 months. Analogously, we estimate MES using 12-month rolling (daily) data, different from Acharya *et al.* (2017). While Kreis and Leisen (2018) use 3-month rolling (daily) data, we use 12-month rolling (data) here. Subject to estimation error, 12-month rolling windows provide a description of these measures over time that captures indirectly a conditioning on the market environment.

The calculation of SRISK requires accounting data that was unavailable to us. While not directly comparable with the banks in our sample, we use aggregate worldwide SRISK based on the individual SRISK measure that the Volatility Laboratory of the Stern Volatility Institute at New York University provides for a worldwide sample (https://vlab.stern.nyu.edu). SRISK is a monetary value, but we are mostly interested in the temporal evolution; to make it comparable in scale to the other measures, we rescaled SRISK such that it equals 1/10 in March 2009. (At that date SRISK has a maximum over the time period.)

When we discuss systemic risk measures for the world financial system and (separately) for the financial systems of each geographical region, we use the banks in the respective area (subject to the above data cleaning procedure). We first determine banks' individual risk contributions ΔCoVaR$_i$ and MES$_i$ as well as individual loadings and then aggregate them to a risk measure of the entire system as described in Equations (6.4, 6.5, 6.10). We proceed analogously with SRISK, see Equation (6.6). Note that ΔCEDF is defined at the aggregate level.

In Section 7.4 of this Chapter, we discuss systemic risk country by country. Some countries have only a small number of banks, and we eliminate those that have only a single bank left. Also, many countries have such a small number of banks that we consider it inappropriate to determine a market return for further analysis. For stability in these cases and for comparability across countries, we choose in Section 7.4 to determine individual bank risk measures (MES, ΔCoVaR, loadings, and ΔCEDF) under the

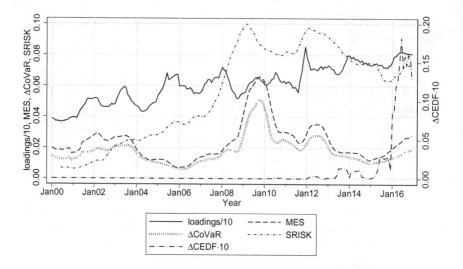

Fig. 7.1: Monthly evolution of the main systemic risk measures in the 21st century, World financial sector.

assumption that they are all part of the same worldwide financial system. We then aggregate them as described above to country-level systemic risk measures.

7.2 Worldwide systemic risk

This section treats banks worldwide as a single financial system, i.e., we look jointly at all 578 banks in our dataset as a single financial sector. To simplify the discussion, we present rolling 6-month averages over (calculated, monthly) values of all risk measures. Figure 7.1 plots the monthly evolution of the five systemic risk measures for the world financial sector. The left scale applies to loadings (rescaled to a tenth), MES, ΔCoVaR, and rescaled SRISK; the right-hand scale applies to ΔCEDF (rescaled by 10).

We see that MES and ΔCoVaR move mostly close in line and that *MES* is always larger than ΔCoVaR. These two observations confirm the conjectures in Section 6.4. Both measures increase (strongly) around the Lehman default (September 15, 2008) and peak afterwards around September 2009.[1] Another peak appears around May 2012, when the Euro crisis

---

[1] Recall that we use rolling 12-month averages to determine both measures and that we plot 6-month rolling averages of the so-calculated values; thus, any date includes events up to 18 months before that date.

culminated. (The second Greek bailout was in March 2012, and a 50% haircut was implemented in April 2012.) After that the readings of both measures decrease. While they increase somewhat since 2015, at the end of our data period they are essentially back to levels seen at the beginning of the current century. Overall, these two measures suggest that current systemic risk has been contained after the Lehman default and the ensuing financial crisis has passed.

The SRISK measure starts increasing earlier, since 2001 at least. The rate of the increase gets stronger with the beginning of 2007, and the measure peaks in March 2009. From a world financial sector perspective, this increase suggests that SRISK would have served well to inform of imminent stress before the global financial crisis. This confirms Brownlees and Engle (2016), who advocate the use of SRISK as an early-warning signal. Similar to ΔCoVaR and MES, SRISK peaks again in early 2012 (Greek crisis). Since 2009, SRISK has gone slightly down but not as much as ΔCoVaR and MES. While the latter suggest that systemic risk is contained at the end of our observation period, SRISK shows it at levels seen just before the GFC.

Over the course of the last 17 years, average loadings have increased from roughly 40% to 80%, following an upward trend over the years. At the end of 2016, worldwide loadings are at an all-time high, suggesting that the worldwide financial system is more integrated than over the previous 15 years.

In terms of the ΔCEDF measure, the years before 2016 appear essentially flat in our scale due to the non-linear dependence of ΔCEDF on loadings (average, heterogeneity). Focusing on the period up to the Lehman event, one would clearly see this as a peak in ΔCEDF. Focusing on the sub-period up to the end of 2013 (not presented here), one would see temporary peaks in the ΔCEDF measure in August 2011 and in February-March 2012.

According to ΔCEDF (and in line with SRISK), systemic risk is currently at an all-time high, even much higher than during the GFC. As discussed in Chapter 6, the ΔCEDF measure is larger when the heterogeneity in loadings or the number of banks is smaller. Though the number of banks in our dataset changes over the course of the years, these changes are small. However, the heterogeneity in loadings (not presented here) has decreased considerably since 2015.

7.3 Systemic risk across geographical regions

This section splits the world into six regions: (1) North America (Canada, United States); (2) Latin America (Argentina, Brazil, Chile, Mexico); (3) Europe[2]; (4) Asia; (5) Australia; (6) Africa and the Middle East. Our analysis treats these six regions as six separate banking systems. We calculate MES, ΔCoVaR and loadings for each individual bank in the respective banking system and aggregate them, as described before, at each month over the time period 2000–2016. Analogously, we determine monthly ΔCEDF but do not have to aggregate as it already characterizes the entire system. To simplify the discussion, we plot rolling 6-month averages over the so-calculated averages. We do not present SRISK because the V-Lab at New York University provides this data for download at the worldwide level but not at our regional level and because we do not have access to the necessary accounting data to implement it ourselves.

Our insights derived for MES and ΔCoVaR at the worldwide level (Section 7.2) remain valid in all six figures (Figures 7.2–7.7): First, MES and ΔCoVaR move closely in line, and MES is always larger than ΔCoVaR. Second, the two major financial crises of the last years (GFC, Euro crisis) show up as peaks for these two measures (with the exception of the Euro crisis for the African/Middle East financial sector).

The temporal evolution of loadings for the regions of North America, Europe, Asia, and Australia are all similar and are also similar to that for the world financial system: They have increased steadily over the years. An exception to this is Europe: Initially, average loadings have decreased considerably since the Euro crisis and reached a temporary minimum between mid-2014 and mid-2015 at roughly 60%. Since then it has increased strongly again, almost up to the levels before the Euro crisis. In Latin America and Africa/Middle East, the loadings measure moves sideways (with a lot of variation across years).

Quantitatively, loadings have remained high since the mid-2000s and are even higher currently (almost 90%) in the U.S. than internationally; loadings are somewhat smaller in the Latin American, Asian, and African-Middle East regions than in the North American, European, and Australian financial regions.

---

[2]One might want to distinguish between countries that have the Euro currency and those that did not adopt it. However, there are only slight differences between the Euro and Non-Euro financial sectors, the only difference being quantitatively that all measures show higher readings in the Euro area compared to the non-Euro area. Thus, we present these here together.

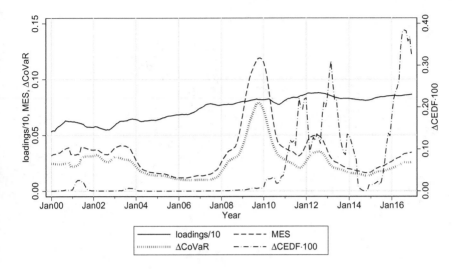

Fig. 7.2: Monthly evolution of the main systemic risk measures in the 21st century, North American financial sector.

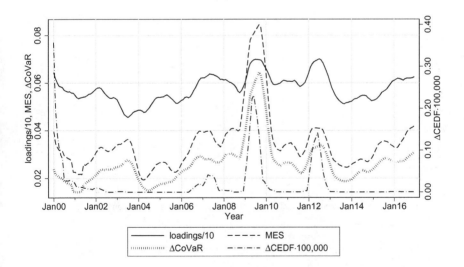

Fig. 7.3: Monthly evolution of the main systemic risk measures in the 21st century, Latin America financial sector.

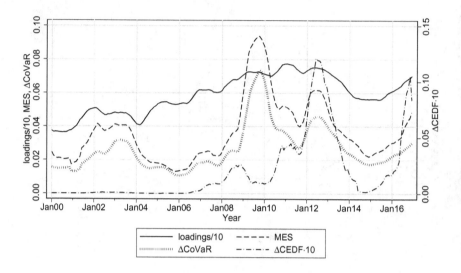

Fig. 7.4: Monthly evolution of the main systemic risk measures in the 21st century, European financial sector.

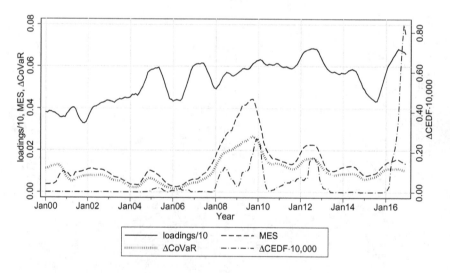

Fig. 7.5: Monthly evolution of the main systemic risk measures in the 21st century, Asian financial sector.

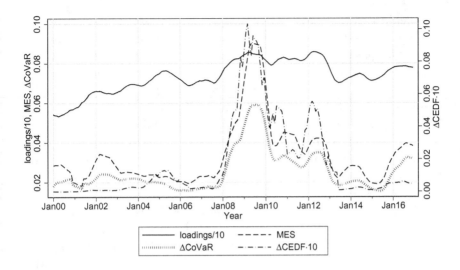

Fig. 7.6: Monthly evolution of the main systemic risk measures in the 21st century, Australian financial sector.

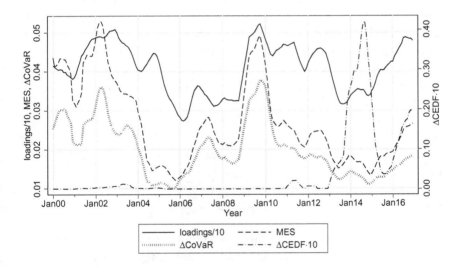

Fig. 7.7: Monthly evolution of the main systemic risk measures in the 21st century, Africa/Middle East financial sector.

The ΔCEDF measure shows that systemic risk has increased considerably over the last 15 years in North America, Europe, and Africa/Middle East. This pales in comparison with the Lehman events; yet, this is due to scale: on a smaller scale, the crisis following the Lehman bankruptcy clearly shows up. It is important to stress that the ΔCEDF measure for these three regions is much larger since 2011, particularly in 2016. This implication about systemic risk is different from MES and ΔCoVaR, which both show current systemic risk to be at pre-GFC levels. Overall, for these three regions, the insight is the same as the one with respect to the world financial sector.

Some differences in ΔCEDF across regions are worth pointing out. Figure 7.2 displays the four systemic risk measures for North America (USA and Canada). Here, the ΔCEDF shows that systemic risk in North America is higher during the Euro crisis than during the GFC and reaches unprecedented levels during 2016. The readings of the ΔCEDF measure in this Figure 7.2 are about 20% of that in the world financial sector of Figure 7.1, showing that systemic risk of North America (as a financial system) is quantitatively smaller than systemic risk of the worldwide financial system. In Europe, the ΔCEDF measure is comparable to the worldwide measure; it clearly shows the Lehman event but the Euro crisis shows up more strongly under this measure. Moreover, this measure suggests that currently systemic risk in Europe is at all-time highs.

For the other three regions (Latin America, Asia, and Australia), we find that current ΔCEDF is contained. For Australia, the readings are much smaller than for North America and Europe. In terms of scale, the ΔCEDF in Latin America and Asia is significantly smaller than in the world and North American financial sectors but not so in the African/Middle East region. Overall, the readings suggest that systemic risk is currently not a major concern across these three regions.

7.4   Systemic risk across countries

After studying the monthly evolution of systemic risk across six geographical regions of the world, we now study it across the years 2000–2016 in a country-by-country comparison. To save space, we do not provide figures showing the temporal evolution of each of the four systemic risk measures separately for each country. Instead, we present four separate tables (Tables 7.2–7.5) that show (average) yearly risk measures for the countries. For several of the 51 countries, the risk measures could not be calculated for any bank, and these countries have been eliminated.

Table 7.2: Presenting $\Delta CoVaR_{system}$ (multiplied by 1,000) across countries and years.

Country	\multicolumn{17}{c}{Years}

Country	00	01	02	03	04	05	06	07	08	09	10	11	12	13	14	15	16
Abu Dhabi								3.3	8.3	9.8				11.1	1.5	10.6	13.2
Argentina	9.5	8.9	2.8		14.0	12.8	12.8	18.6	17.0	24.9	20.6	23.9	20.2	13.7	24.4	30.0	18.8
Australia	4.4	2.1	5.1	1.8	9.6	8.4	7.1	13.0	22.0	44.5	22.3	22.1	26.9	29.6	11.4	10.5	18.5
Austria	5.5	10.8	14.0	12.3	10.4	8.6	15.4	26.0	32.4	86.9	49.0	38.0	44.9		23.2	23.3	26.6
Bahrain						0.5		1.0		3.2		0.7			1.0	6.1	2.4
Belgium	8.6	10.5	16.8	16.8	11.2	9.2	15.5	20.4	33.5	90.1	57.7	41.8	49.0	31.2	20.3	16.8	20.4
Brazil	11.7	15.8	12.7	8.9	14.7	16.3	24.4	31.0	29.5	57.9	23.3	24.5	28.6	18.6	17.8	24.2	30.8
Canada	13.1	16.1	14.4	12.2	8.8	7.2	6.8	8.9	19.1	44.4	22.1	16.9	20.4	12.2	7.7	12.3	16.9
Chile						0.2		3.7	15.5	25.9	9.8	16.4	25.1	8.3	9.2	6.7	14.1
China							0.1	11.4	23.1	32.6	13.7	13.6	17.2	10.8	7.0	8.7	10.5
Denmark	6.2	7.3	10.0	7.7	7.2	6.8	11.9	16.9	24.8	43.1	32.9	29.1	34.2	18.1	14.5	13.7	18.7
Egypt	3.2	2.9	6.8	0.3	0.3	3.3	16.5	16.6	11.4	22.1	13.4	6.9	2.5		1.9	9.6	13.5
France	6.4	19.0	21.7	35.2	18.5	11.5	17.5	20.5	29.5	57.4	42.2	47.2	60.8	37.1	21.6	20.4	29.1
Germany	11.0	23.2	36.1	34.5	20.4	10.9	17.6	22.5	29.3	71.2	40.8	37.0	54.6	35.7	20.9	16.3	28.6
Greece	4.0	8.2	10.9	4.8	9.7	8.8	14.4	18.7	24.3	51.4	41.6	24.2	15.3	29.7	20.9	37.3	40.3
HongKong	4.9	7.8	8.0	2.3	4.2	1.9	2.5	10.0	13.5	26.2	9.3	10.0	16.0	5.5	4.7	7.8	15.6
India	3.2	3.8	7.0	2.7	8.2	12.5	13.5	17.2	20.3	29.5	20.5	14.3	14.9	12.8	18.1	13.2	16.1
Ireland	5.2	5.8	13.4	14.9	9.1	6.4	11.2	16.8	37.3	87.8	53.3	47.5	42.6	37.0	22.2	17.1	32.2
Israel	8.7	9.3	7.0	6.7	7.0	6.3	9.2	14.8	15.5	23.5	15.7	17.8	23.1	10.9	7.9	5.2	11.8
Italy	7.0	12.8	19.7	23.1	11.5	9.1	13.0	15.6	23.2	54.6	38.3	43.1	56.4	37.4	23.5	23.1	29.8

(*Continued*)

Table 7.2: (*Continued*)

	00	01	02	03	04	05	06	07	08	09	10	11	12	13	14	15	16
Japan	0.2	7.5	7.0	1.3	12.1	6.9	9.5	9.0	11.8	19.1	1.4	2.1	0.9	1.5	2.5	1.4	2.4
Kuwait						1.4	2.6	1.5	1.6	11.3	1.7	1.9	3.6	0.9		3.7	9.1
Malaysia	0.3	11.1					3.0	13.0	12.5	14.4	10.6	9.8	7.3	4.4	6.1	10.2	11.0
Mexico	10.8		12.2	13.1	7.3	8.9	13.5	13.0	11.5	33.3	20.9	19.5	26.6	17.2	14.5	15.5	16.7
Morocco		4.5				1.3	6.9	3.5	2.1	8.7	6.0	9.4	9.1	7.8	2.3		1.8
Norway	4.3	6.8	12.8	7.6	8.8	5.5	13.8	18.0	23.3	74.6	31.6	28.5	38.3	23.3	15.0	19.2	24.2
Oman						4.6	1.2	5.7	3.9	20.8	7.5	6.2	2.1	2.7	1.9	10.4	9.2
Pakistan					2.7	2.4	1.0	3.0	3.9	0.7	0.3	1.4		2.0	2.8	0.3	3.9
Philippines	3.0	0.4	4.1	1.2	2.0	7.2	5.6	13.2	17.4	16.9	7.5	8.7	9.7	9.4	11.9	2.2	7.6
Poland	6.7	5.5		2.8	8.1	8.0	14.1	19.6	24.9	51.9	35.3	30.8	34.6	15.6	12.4	11.3	19.6
Portugal	2.5	6.4	12.0	8.2	8.7		7.4	13.1	23.9	29.9	33.5	35.0	39.8	19.9	26.0	27.1	23.3
Qatar						1.3	0.1	4.7	7.3	18.2	8.5	7.0	4.4	1.3	2.4	6.6	10.9
Russia	18.0	5.8	5.2	3.6	9.3	12.0	21.9	26.0	27.0	71.3	41.3	26.7	38.9	23.7	26.6	35.4	30.4
Singapore	6.9	6.9	9.5	5.1	11.3	6.0	8.5	16.3	19.0	28.9	15.5	16.0	22.5	10.1	7.1	7.4	10.7
South Africa	7.3	10.5	8.3	8.0	9.0	13.8	23.2	30.0	27.0	53.2	27.0	23.4	22.8	13.2	15.9	16.9	25.8
Spain	8.6	17.4	22.9	26.2	16.9	10.9	12.9	17.8	24.8	51.8	38.1	35.6	40.1	35.5	21.8	20.2	30.2
Sweden	5.4	10.9	24.4	27.2	15.0	11.1	17.0	22.0	23.1	51.8	36.7	33.5	39.3	20.6	16.3	12.4	19.6
Switzerland	2.5	2.9	0.7	2.4	3.9	4.9	7.4	16.6	15.4	15.9	13.1	18.4	25.2	14.1	10.5	7.1	14.1
Taiwan	3.8	8.0	3.8	2.8	6.4	5.9	4.8	5.3	6.8	11.5	9.9	8.5	8.8	3.0	1.0	3.0	4.8
Thailand	4.8	1.5	7.6	2.8	4.7	6.8	8.9	14.5	11.0	24.6	8.5	11.4	15.8	10.9	10.6	6.4	11.5
Turkey	14.3	32.8	23.7	22.9	14.7	13.7	22.8	32.2	34.6	54.2	29.8	29.5	28.6	19.6	22.2	12.6	20.3
UK	17.9	18.7	25.7	22.9	14.7	9.2	11.8	16.1	29.8	65.1	37.3	28.7	36.5	19.5	11.6	13.7	26.7
USA	22.2	25.6	23.8	25.6	11.9	7.6	5.2	10.4	23.2	72.8	30.6	24.8	31.2	14.4	10.7	13.5	19.6

Table 7.3: Presenting MES$_{system}$ (multiplied by 1,000) across countries and years.

Country	Years																
	00	01	02	03	04	05	06	07	08	09	10	11	12	13	14	15	16
Abu Dhabi	14.9							0.9	8.3	16.3	0.0				0.6	8.0	22.0
Argentina	9.0	12.6	15.4		18.4	19.6	13.7	22.3	26.9	45.0	27.1	26.7	34.3	14.5	27.9	26.6	28.8
Australia	4.1	3.1	6.4	6.2	11.7	13.4	12.9	18.3	32.0	55.0	31.1	29.1	30.0	17.2	12.7	10.3	23.7
Austria		13.7	11.9	17.4	11.6	12.5	23.1	29.5	46.7	103.7	62.9	49.8	67.0	40.4	27.7	33.2	30.6
Bahrain							0.1	1.4	0.3	3.8		0.8	0.5			0.5	3.4
Belgium	11.3	20.9	22.9	22.3	14.7	14.1	22.6	26.3	43.4	94.0	65.8	51.4	71.6	40.2	23.5	21.8	30.5
Brazil	21.7	19.2	25.0	14.5	22.3	22.6	30.0	33.0	45.7	69.6	34.0	32.4	40.4	22.0	23.9	32.0	31.6
Canada	18.2	23.8	19.8	17.2	9.2	9.6	7.2	12.2	29.1	64.8	31.2	23.2	25.4	12.2	9.3	17.4	23.5
Chile						0.2		4.7	21.7	37.1	16.3	19.4	30.9	10.8	13.7	14.0	15.6
China							0.1	12.9	35.4	49.2	15.0	18.5	24.9	14.5	10.8	10.0	21.7
Denmark	8.3	19.4	21.5	16.0	7.8	10.4	18.3	22.8	41.8	77.4	38.8	34.7	44.2	26.2	14.1	17.2	24.4
Egypt	6.0	10.5	3.2	1.6	5.6		11.0	17.7	10.2	32.2	16.6	10.6	2.2		4.7	7.1	14.8
France	13.6	32.6	31.2	41.5	21.3	15.0	20.5	25.9	45.8	79.7	59.2	58.4	76.5	41.4	24.6	28.6	43.2
Germany	13.0	34.1	40.9	47.2	25.0	15.4	22.3	27.7	49.7	102.9	51.7	47.7	71.3	39.7	22.8	25.7	45.5
Greece	11.3	14.6	8.0	8.7	18.5	11.7	18.4	22.9	38.3	54.8	47.1	45.5	53.2	41.0	30.1	37.8	45.4
Hong Kong	5.0	5.7	5.3	2.1	7.0	3.2	3.2	12.4	26.1	38.6	8.3	11.1	16.9	9.2	8.2	11.1	19.8
India		2.3	7.3	2.6	14.5	13.2	16.4	19.2	31.5	54.9	21.8	17.0	23.9	19.3	23.6	17.9	26.9
Ireland	11.7	19.6	22.3	22.3	10.0	10.3	13.2	24.8	60.7	91.1	74.9	53.9	46.3	33.5	16.5	25.9	41.4
Israel	11.7	16.5	11.7	8.5	6.4	6.2	14.7	17.7	22.5	37.6	25.4	22.0	29.2	14.8	9.2	6.2	15.5
Italy	10.5	20.9	25.9	24.1	12.1	9.7	16.0	19.5	33.9	69.4	54.2	49.0	61.7	40.4	26.5	30.7	47.0

(Continued)

Table 7.3: (Continued)

	00	01	02	03	04	05	06	07	08	09	10	11	12	13	14	15	16
Japan	4.8	8.1	16.9	4.4	11.0	6.5	12.6	11.9	17.1	34.7	1.7	1.8	1.0	2.4	2.2	1.4	3.8
Kuwait						1.5				5.8	3.3	3.8	4.9	0.9	0.4	4.7	9.7
Malaysia	0.2						4.5	15.4	14.6	23.7	11.6	9.9	10.3	5.7	6.8	14.5	14.0
Mexico	19.4	17.7	18.1	16.6	8.7	9.7	15.7	18.2	18.6	43.3	27.4	24.3	32.6	20.3	21.0	17.4	30.2
Morocco	0.5	4.9				3.8	8.0	1.1	6.0	15.9	6.4	6.4	7.5	3.9	0.3	0.1	0.9
Norway	10.4	15.0	16.1	15.4	10.1	9.5	20.6	23.3	40.1	97.9	52.7	41.5	52.1	27.7	17.5	20.5	36.0
Oman							0.3	3.0	2.5	25.6	8.0	6.0	3.1	3.5	2.9	11.5	8.8
Pakistan		0.0			0.5			4.1	5.3	0.8	3.3	0.7		3.8	4.6	4.2	6.0
Philippines	2.0	2.9	1.3	1.7	5.1	11.1	2.4	15.6	14.9	25.6	6.1	6.6	8.6	12.0	12.4	2.3	6.2
Poland	7.2	16.6	10.4	6.3	8.5		22.9	25.2	38.1	73.1	47.5	37.3	44.6	23.0	16.6	12.2	23.4
Portugal	6.8	13.2	19.9	16.1	10.1	8.9	6.7	17.7	31.6	45.0	41.7	40.0	49.9	32.2	27.9	29.9	28.1
Qatar						0.5	7.0	3.0	3.1	21.9	5.1	5.9	2.8	1.1	2.3	5.5	13.8
Russia	20.3	13.7		3.8	13.5	6.9	33.7	35.0	42.6	89.7	54.4	42.0	53.0	34.4	28.9	31.9	39.3
Singapore	15.5	11.6	12.2	5.5	17.3	9.5	10.4	19.7	27.3	44.1	19.1	18.0	27.6	14.1	10.0	10.7	18.7
South Africa	21.1	15.2	16.9	13.5	7.7	14.7	30.1	38.9	35.9	46.9	34.9	29.3	35.7	23.0	22.0	15.8	37.6
Spain	13.6	30.1	31.4	30.6	21.4	16.8	17.2	21.4	36.2	74.0	53.9	45.0	46.5	35.8	26.5	27.0	39.2
Sweden	11.4	29.2	34.8	31.0	16.9	13.4	19.5	27.4	39.5	83.1	52.1	44.1	54.6	25.8	17.9	14.5	31.2
Switzerland	3.1	4.6	1.5		3.9	6.4	7.3	16.3	19.5	22.0	16.9	26.1	34.6	17.9	11.6	12.8	22.6
Taiwan		7.6	3.9	3.5	9.0	9.3	5.5	6.6	10.2	24.0	11.0	9.2	9.7	4.4	1.4	6.5	8.7
Thailand	16.5	7.4	5.9	8.7	8.8	8.3	11.2	14.5	19.3	40.2	7.5	10.2	19.0	17.5	12.6	11.4	16.9
Turkey		38.3	32.9	9.6	26.9	26.0	35.3	44.2	49.1	55.6	36.8	33.3	38.0	24.5	29.3	16.5	23.6
UK	23.9	27.6	31.4	23.0	15.9	10.4	13.5	19.4	43.7	85.1	52.5	36.2	45.2	24.6	16.6	21.1	42.6
USA	31.9	34.3	33.3	32.9	11.9	7.5	5.1	9.8	29.3	93.0	48.7	31.6	39.1	15.3	14.1	20.3	31.2

Table 7.4: Presenting average factor loadings (multiplied by 100) across countries and years.

Country	Years																
	00	01	02	03	04	05	06	07	08	09	10	11	12	13	14	15	16
Abu Dhabi	42.3	57.5	18.9	39.4	24.9	4.3	39.9	50.3	47.2	53.7	52.6	54.6	86.4	64.6	90.2	63.6	58.5
Argentina	30.7	28.1	52.7	49.1	32.6	35.4	45.3	52.3	41.4	65.6	45.8	42.5	48.6	44.8	65.0	76.5	74.4
Australia	16.7	26.3	44.7	51.9	51.8	51.3	64.7	65.7	47.5	69.4	50.0	47.8	74.2		50.6	57.9	85.8
Austria						35.5	75.1	78.6	48.6	60.1	49.9	45.3		89.2	82.3	67.7	81.8
Bahrain	38.6	38.1	38.0	52.2	47.1	44.3	46.4	43.6	42.6	47.1			30.7	41.2	63.4	48.4	29.3
Belgium	49.6	44.8	37.7	42.1	43.5	44.7	54.2	78.5	53.8	62.1	56.5	53.2	46.9	63.3	68.5	69.3	68.8
Brazil	55.4	50.3	48.3	46.3	43.0	56.1	55.6	62.5	55.2	76.0	73.3	63.2	83.9	69.3	71.6	54.9	81.4
Canada						57.9	57.3	59.8	56.6	64.9	49.2	60.3	82.0	67.2	68.4	86.8	80.9
Chile								29.3	49.7	77.9	38.0	65.7	45.8	67.2	84.0	74.4	77.7
China								55.7	55.3	70.2	65.1	42.7	28.3	41.6	39.4	54.1	83.4
Denmark	24.4	29.6	35.6	39.8	29.6	50.9	73.7	79.7	53.7	72.1	62.0	55.6	67.6	65.1	58.2	64.8	70.3
Egypt	20.5	15.9	31.6	27.1	26.3	36.5	49.4	47.5	52.8	63.8	68.3	48.4	28.7	66.5	53.7	56.3	50.3
France	22.3	57.5	81.7	67.3	27.7	48.6	66.7	81.3	53.5	65.1	77.2	83.3	58.1	80.9	82.2	77.4	86.0
Germany	18.7	45.0	75.8	37.5	37.6	32.7	62.3	77.5	53.3	67.1	74.7	63.5	82.1	82.5	83.9	73.6	84.8
Greece	25.4	37.4	54.3	51.7	30.9	58.3	69.6	77.7	55.7	48.0	58.2	47.8	48.5	63.6	75.7	59.6	62.6
Hong Kong	23.1	30.0	34.5	24.1	19.5	50.6	58.6	63.0	53.4	63.6	67.5	47.5	46.0	49.1	42.5	42.6	72.4
India	20.4	24.8	25.6	27.9	23.5	37.8	57.7	55.6	52.1	76.5	52.9	41.1	39.9	72.0	84.1	63.0	84.3
Ireland	20.8	32.7	29.6	60.0	22.0	63.5	66.0	78.6	50.0	69.7	65.9	43.9	62.8	54.3	39.6	64.7	81.4
Israel	38.4	31.2	21.2	36.1	30.6	49.1	56.0	78.4	52.4	65.4	72.4	53.7	44.2	68.0	86.7	72.1	76.1
Italy	25.6	39.2	63.7	54.3	37.5	43.6	61.7	69.9	50.0	67.5	77.8	81.1	74.4	66.4	62.1	55.9	81.1

(Continued)

Table 7.4: (*Continued*)

	00	01	02	03	04	05	06	07	08	09	10	11	12	13	14	15	16
Japan	25.7	21.6	25.1	26.7	28.9	31.0	58.7	67.9	33.8	33.4	33.4	49.0	43.7	78.1	65.7	51.9	48.2
Kuwait						62.7	39.4	32.0	36.6	26.4	33.0	36.0	44.9	56.3	59.3	54.2	40.4
Malaysia							42.9	40.7	37.6	58.4	53.8	44.1	28.3	55.1	60.7	68.3	71.3
Mexico	61.3	58.7	20.1	39.8	44.9	57.1	48.3	46.4	44.1	57.6	58.0	44.8	63.4	68.0	82.6	77.4	71.0
Morocco	14.6	16.6	17.7	39.4	38.6	44.5	52.7	49.9	38.7	29.4	31.1	44.2	42.4	38.4	53.7	31.5	40.8
Norway	24.1	45.0	52.7	32.7	25.1	49.9	61.5	73.6	52.1	62.4	49.2	46.5	63.5	71.5	56.4	84.4	83.7
Oman							9.1	43.1	46.2	48.9	37.2	39.5	51.8	67.9	61.1	49.4	52.2
Pakistan	26.8	29.8	26.7	6.7	26.5	59.1	40.6	46.0	32.8	15.8	43.4	38.7	38.3	55.9	63.3	54.2	61.0
Philippines	19.7	20.5	24.4	48.2	19.1	29.3	57.0	73.1	40.7	45.4	44.0	43.0	55.2	70.1	76.3	67.3	64.8
Poland	27.7	50.0	74.1	33.2	26.9	49.5	54.3	53.2	50.8	56.2	73.5	65.0	67.8	64.7	59.6	63.3	78.0
Portugal				67.2	49.9	36.0	47.8	58.0	35.9	62.1	80.6	75.7	33.1	45.7	51.9	59.9	60.4
Qatar						67.2	33.2	38.4	54.1	59.0	33.6	33.4	34.5	68.6	78.9	72.1	44.7
Russia	12.3	16.4	13.3	40.1	24.7	20.5	44.6	64.5	47.5	66.1	52.0	47.3	85.0	80.6	82.8	77.6	77.4
Singapore	26.3	34.6	24.5	48.1	31.0	47.0	70.4	78.5	39.2	62.5	68.6	51.1	46.8	69.1	86.2	77.0	92.7
South Africa	21.4	39.8	39.6	40.1	21.7	38.3	55.0	64.2	40.8	26.3	55.7	36.6	68.6	71.2	71.1	73.5	83.5
Spain	32.7	51.5	71.9	63.5	32.3	35.3	61.9	83.7	56.9	75.4	75.6	74.8	66.1	80.0	77.0	65.2	82.7
Sweden	36.2	36.5	63.8	71.2	30.2	45.5	76.8	81.6	56.1	75.6	81.1	77.1	76.5	85.3	78.7	83.3	85.3
Switzerland	21.3	22.0	25.3	22.4	37.1	29.4	57.6	61.7	38.0	33.5	43.8	38.8	58.9	64.6	62.5	63.3	69.7
Taiwan	34.1	31.1	21.3	18.8	22.5	32.6	41.9	64.1	43.8	45.3	59.7	40.3	54.5	39.6	57.6	79.3	75.2
Thailand	21.0	25.0	35.2	33.4	29.6	34.3	46.3	61.2	37.5	65.5	70.6	44.8	32.8	61.6	70.0	77.2	83.9
Turkey	43.6	26.7	23.5	34.4	21.4	36.7	53.0	74.5	51.2	67.8	70.1	48.7	63.4	81.0	78.7	54.1	81.9
UK	40.2	47.8	68.4	64.1	23.7	48.5	56.7	77.0	55.6	65.5	72.4	59.3	68.2	76.6	78.2	78.5	80.8
USA	60.4	64.3	55.3	55.5	65.7	67.2	50.0	51.0	73.3	63.2	62.7	81.5	87.8	87.9	89.1	91.3	92.3

Table 7.5: Presenting ΔCEDF (multiplied by 1,000) across countries and years.

Country	Years																
	00	01	02	03	04	05	06	07	08	09	10	11	12	13	14	15	16
Abu Dhabi	0.0					5.3	0.1	13.0	0.1	0.0	25.9	0.1				2.0	0.6
Argentina	0.0	47.4	7.4	0.0	0.0	0.3	0.0	0.1	0.0	0.0	0.0	0.0	13.7	0.7	0.3	1.9	2.5
Australia	0.0	0.0	0.0	0.0	0.0	0.0	0.7	1.0	0.0	0.5	0.0	0.0	0.0	0.0	0.0	0.0	3.5
Austria						44.0	68.8	172.8	18.8	38.9	34.8	27.8	151.8	166.4	119.3	96.1	244.9
Bahrain	9.4	15.6	8.2	11.6	20.9	43.7	21.8	13.5	0.9	2.5		37.8	7.7	23.9	5.8	1.1	9.8
Belgium	0.0					0.6	35.3	94.9	13.1	37.1	42.5	34.2	19.4	48.0	53.0	49.8	84.4
Brazil	0.0	0.0	0.0	0.0	0.0	0.0	0.0	0.2	0.0	8.8	0.0	0.0	3.1	0.2	0.7	0.0	31.4
Canada	0.0	0.0	0.0	0.0	0.0		0.0	0.0	0.0	0.0	0.0	0.0	0.6	0.0	0.0	6.2	1.3
Chile								25.5	27.7	75.6	25.6	34.7	52.0	57.0	86.2	90.8	111.5
China								1.1	0.0	0.2	0.0	0.0	0.0	0.0	0.0	0.0	5.6
Denmark	0.0	0.0	0.0	0.0	0.0	1.7	6.3	8.9	0.0	0.9	0.7	0.3	5.8	0.4	0.0	0.9	4.0
Egypt	6.7	18.5	18.5	16.4	9.0	14.0	18.0	3.3	3.0	11.3	7.0	2.0	30.8	44.3	25.6	12.0	20.9
France	5.7	71.5	15.6	13.4	0.2	0.4	16.2	38.6	0.6	15.1	35.7	65.7	15.6	90.5	90.9	54.2	125.7
Germany	0.0	49.0	78.4	0.4	0.8	1.4	6.3	45.0	0.7	15.2	18.6	5.7	66.3	55.2	48.1	36.5	23.7
Greece	0.1	0.0	0.1	0.2	0.0	1.1	7.8	6.8	0.2	0.2	0.1	0.0	1.0	1.9	2.2	3.5	2.0
HK	0.0	0.7	0.2	0.3	0.2	90.3	10.3	0.3	0.0	0.0	0.1	0.1	0.0	0.1	0.0	0.0	1.5
India	0.0	0.0	0.0	0.0	0.0	0.1	0.3	0.9	0.0	1.4	0.1	0.0	0.0	1.6	4.8	0.1	30.8
Ireland	7.2	29.6	16.1	36.0	7.9	189.3	88.7	103.9	14.0	58.5	54.1	26.5	50.9	18.7	27.3	65.9	117.0
Israel	0.0	0.0	0.0	0.0	0.0	2.1	0.8	5.0	0.0	0.3	0.7	0.0	0.0	1.2	5.7	1.1	3.5
Italy	0.0	0.0	0.0	0.0	0.0	0.0	0.0	0.1	0.0	0.0	0.4	0.1	0.0	0.0	0.0	0.0	1.8

(Continued)

Table 7.5: (Continued)

	00	01	02	03	04	05	06	07	08	09	10	11	12	13	14	15	16
Japan	0.0	0.0	0.0	0.0	0.0	0.0	0.1	4.5	0.0	0.0	0.0	0.0	0.1	0.0	0.0	0.0	0.0
Kuwait				0.0	41.1	0.0	0.0	0.0	0.0	0.0	0.0	0.0	0.0	0.0	0.0	0.0	0.0
Malaysia							0.0	0.0	0.0	0.0	0.0	0.0	0.0	0.0	0.0	0.0	0.1
Mexico	4.7	1.5	0.2	0.8	1.2	49.7	2.8	3.8	0.1	0.2	2.2	0.3	0.1	1.8	5.4	3.5	1.6
Morocco	0.1	0.1	0.0	20.9	0.3	2.1	0.4	1.0	0.0	0.0	0.0	0.1	0.0	0.0	1.1	0.0	0.0
Norw.	0.0	0.2	0.3	0.0	0.0	3.2	1.5	14.1	0.1	0.5	0.2	0.7	3.5	4.7	0.1	14.4	40.1
Oman																	
Pakistan	0.1	0.0	7.3	0.0	12.1	0.1	0.0	0.1	0.0	0.0	0.0	0.0	0.0	0.0	0.0	0.0	0.0
Philippines	0.0	0.0	0.0	0.1	0.1	1.8	2.7	2.4	0.0	0.0	0.0	0.0	0.1	0.2	0.1	0.0	0.0
Poland					0.0	0.3	0.0	0.0	0.0	0.2	0.2	0.0	0.1	0.2	0.0	0.1	0.5
Portugal	11.7	53.0	93.8	44.4	16.6	21.4	26.8	78.0	9.5	45.0	130.4	135.8	16.6	30.2	22.1	62.1	27.2
Qatar						0.6	0.0	0.2	0.1	0.1	0.0	0.0	0.0	0.2	21.5	0.1	0.0
Russia	5.9	5.9	8.4	24.0	7.3	147.6	20.1	72.3	45.8	75.5	43.9	27.2	152.4	111.1	127.9	26.7	178.5
Singapore	0.2	0.3	0.1	2.3	0.3	0.8	24.5	30.2	0.7	5.9	8.5	2.0	4.5	10.8	22.4	29.7	166.2
S. Africa	0.0	0.1	1.1	0.0	0.0	0.0	0.1	0.5	0.0	0.0	0.3	0.0	1.5	0.5	3.1	5.8	17.6
Spain	0.0	1.6	1.1	0.5	0.0	1.0	1.2	22.2	0.0	1.8	1.3	0.6	0.9	2.7	1.1	0.6	10.9
Sweden	0.0	0.1	0.2	0.4	0.0	0.0	2.8	13.1	0.0	5.2	1.7	3.5	12.5	10.6	9.7	5.4	16.5
Switz.	7.3	18.4	0.1	0.1	0.5	13.6	2.2	4.9	0.0	0.0	0.0	0.0	0.8	0.9	0.0	0.0	0.7
Taiwan	0.0	0.0	0.1	0.1	0.0	0.1	0.0	0.1	0.0	0.0	0.0	0.0	0.0	0.0	22.4	12.0	17.1
Thailand	0.0	0.0	0.0	0.0	0.0	0.1	0.0	0.3	0.0	0.0	0.1	0.0	0.0	0.0	0.0	0.5	13.4
Turkey	0.0	0.0	0.0	0.0	0.0	0.0	0.0	0.8	0.0	1.1	0.0	0.0	0.7	1.9	1.9	0.0	2.4
UK	0.0	0.1	0.2	0.1	0.0	0.1	0.1	2.6	0.0	0.1	2.0	0.1	1.5	2.4	2.3	0.1	1.9
USA	0.0	0.0	0.0	0.0	0.0	0.0	0.0	0.0	0.0	0.0	0.0	0.0	2.0	0.0	0.1	14.4	10.2

Table 7.2 presents results of ΔCoVaR for the financial system of each country, multiplied by 1,000 for ease of presentation. While all countries start the new millennium with readings in the single or lower double digits, at the end of our period the readings are usually (medium) double digits and several times that of the initial readings at the beginning. The maximum reading (for each country) is usually attained in 2009, which covers the global financial crisis. (Remember that we use 12-rolling windows to measure systemic risk on a monthly basis then take annual averages; thus, data points in 2009 partially go back to January 2008.)

The minimum of Δ CoVaR (for each country) is usually attained in 2005, which supports the conjectured "volatility puzzle" by Adrian and Brunnermeier (2016): systemic risk is bred in "good" times; during periods of "low" volatility, risk appears too "small," thus tempting banks to take risks that appear excessive afterwards. The last readings (year 2016) are usually lower than during 2009, typically about one-third to one-half of those values. The most notable exceptions are Greece, Italy, and, to a lesser extent, Portugal. In these countries, we clearly see the impact of the Euro crisis in ΔCoVaR. It is important to note, also, that there is a large disparity across readings. In 2016, many countries have readings in the range 10 to 20, including the United States (19.6.); however, several countries also have readings that are much lower, Morocco (1.8) and Bahrain (2.4).

Table 7.3 presents results for MES, also multiplied by 1,000 for ease of presentation. In comparison with ΔCoVaR, we see here, as in Sections 7.2 and 7.3, that MES (usually) has larger values than ΔCoVaR and that both measures move mostly in tandem. In line with that observation, we find here, analogously to ΔCoVaR, that MES usually peaks in 2009 (the GFC), while there is usually a minimum around 2004–2005. In addition, as with ΔCoVaR, the MES readings are, in general, lower at the end of our period compared to the GFC (about one-third to one-half), again Greece, Italy, and Portugal being exceptions.

Quantitatively, the readings of (systemic risk according to) MES during the GFC are economically significant. The presented values of Austria, Germany, Ireland, and the United States are all roughly 100, which translates into roughly 10% expected *relative* loss in value of the banking system.

Table 7.4 presents the loadings, multiplied by 100 for ease of presentation. There are several notable differences to the previous two measures. Most important, the minimum of loadings is some years before the GFC and the maximum is not at the GFC. The readings tend to be fairly small at the beginning of the millennium (usually around 20, corresponding to 20%), but in 2016 they are many times that value (usually around 70–80, corresponding to 70%–80%). (The mathematical maximum is 100, corresponding to 100%.) Some countries continue to exhibit fairly low values in 2016, mostly the Middle Eastern and African countries (Abu Dhabi, Bahrain, Egypt, Kuwait, Morocco) but also Japan. Surprisingly, some banks at the heart of the Euro crisis (Greece, Portugal) have low loadings through many years, including 2016, whereas some other Euro crisis countries (Ireland, Italy, Spain) have significant loadings. Two countries, Singapore and the USA, exhibit particularly large values beyond 90%. For these two countries, the readings are considerably larger than during the GFC. These readings suggest that the interconnectedness of banks in most countries, especially in the USA, has even increased since the GFC despite explicit regulatory concern.

Table 7.5 takes the loadings one step further and presents the ΔCEDF systemic risk measure multiplied by 1,000 for ease of discussion. Recall that this measure takes into account the number of banks. Thus, although the USA and Singapore have high loadings in 2016, the ΔCEDF measure shows that systemic risk in the U.S. is fairly small[3] compared to the other countries here, while it is much larger in Singapore in 2016. Several other countries also had high readings in 2016: Austria, Chile, France, Ireland, and Russia. In general, the readings are higher than in any year before, including the GFC and the Euro crisis; but at times the readings are large just before the GFC. For example, for Austria ΔCEDF is 172.8 in 2007, a value higher than during the Euro crisis (2012–2013) and almost as large as in 2016; for Ireland, the values are 189.3 in 2005, 103.9 in 2007, and 117.0 in 2016; for Russia, the table shows large values at 147.6 in 2005, 152.4 in 2012, values above 100 in 2012–2013, and an even larger value of 178.5 in 2016. Greece does not show up as a major concern, yet Portugal does have high readings just before the Euro crisis, with 130.4 and 135.8 in 2010 and 2011, respectively.

---

[3]For the USA, our table reports 0.0 in most years. Recall that the measure is non-linear, and as loadings have increased considerably over time in the USA, this only shows that systemic risk has been relatively small before 2015–2016, in comparison to 2016. Leaving out these last years, the GFC and Lehman default events show up clearly.

7.5 Main insights

This section briefly summarizes our main insights from this chapter (worldwide, regional, country by country). Keep in mind that (Exposure-) ΔCoVaR and MES were introduced by Adrian and Brunnermeier (2016) and Acharya *et al.* (2017) to measure the *individual* contribution to system risk of a financial institution, whereas here we aggregate this to a systemic risk measure of the financial system, see Chapter 5.

Throughout this chapter, we have seen that MES and ΔCoVaR closely mimic each other, in line with Kupiec and Guntay (2016), and that the former is always larger than the latter. Both measures capture the main systemic risk events that we discussed in Part 1, the global financial crisis and the Euro crisis. They both suggest that systemic risk has been contained worldwide in recent years. Notable exceptions at the end of 2016 are Greece, Italy, and, to a lesser extent, Portugal.

In Section 6.4, we compared these five systemic risk measures theoretically. Under the normality assumption there, we found that MES and ΔCoVaR closely mimic each other and that the former is always larger than the latter. It is surprising that we observe the same here at the worldwide, regional, and country levels since stock return distributions are known to be non-normal. Keep in mind, however, that none of these measures is initially intended to provide a measure of systemic risk for an entire system. Moreover, while both measures mimic each other here, they identified both systemic risk events that occurred between 2000–2016, the GFC and the Euro crisis.

We discussed SRISK only at the level of the worldwide financial system. It also captured the GFC and the Euro crisis but tends to react much earlier before a crisis and might, thus, serve better as an early-warning signal, as discussed by Brownlees and Engle (2016). Different from MES and ΔCoVaR, SRISK has not decreased recently but is, instead, currently at a level comparable to the GFC.

The individual $SRISK_i$ depends on current debt, equity, and long-run MES ($LRMES_i$). As noted in Section 6.4, Brownlees and Engle (2016) report that $LRMES_i$ can be approximated well by normal distribution properties; we then noted after Equation (6.16) that individual $SRISK_i$ would be mostly driven by k, the prudential capital fraction, by debt, equity, and idiosyncratic volatility as well as correlation. Their systemwide SRISK is the total capital *shortfall* of all banks in the system, i.e., it is the total non-negative $SRISK_i$. As such, it is hard to determine what is driving results.

Most important, it provides an important additional view on systemic risk that appears to capture an aspect different from MES and ΔCoVaR.

While loadings and ΔCEDF focus exclusively on interconnectedness. (ΔCEDF considers the impact and, therefore, also takes into account the number of banks in the system.) They provide an additional view on systemic risk that is complementary to MES, ΔCoVaR, and SRISK.

The loadings measure has mostly increased over time in the current century and is usually at all-time highs, thus suggesting that interconnectedness has not decreased but rather increased, despite regulatory efforts. This is in line with Kreis and Leisen (2018), who show for a sample of U.S. banks over the last 36 years that average interconnectedness (loadings) has increased dramatically and heterogeneity has decreased, i.e., banks have become more similar. The ΔCEDF confirms that systemic risk is at all-time highs, which differs from MES and ΔCoVaR, but is in line with SRISK.

PART 3
Regulation

This part discusses prudential regulation and the institutional framework for effective supervision of systemic risk.

Prudential regulation of a financial system faces a series of challenges. As in other industries, regulation in the financial landscape needs to be justified by noting a market failure and determining that public intervention would improve welfare. However, once a market failure has been identified and regulation is deemed necessary, peculiar characteristics of financial markets and financial institutions pose additional challenges to policy-making. We start with Chapter 8 by enumerating these challenges, their potential implications, and solutions.

In Chapter 9, we focus on two perspectives to prudential regulation: micro-prudential and macro-prudential. Prior to the global financial crisis (GFC), the general view among policymakers was micro-prudential: making financial institutions "safe and sound" individually would suffice to guarantee the stability of the whole financial system. The crisis shows that this is not enough; it highlights that the risks of the entire financial system must be analyzed as a unit, a macro-prudential perspective.

Even optimally designed prudential regulation cannot prevent the failure of all financial institutions. Some failures can still occur, and resolution policies are particularly important in such cases. Resolution policies are necessary after a failure occurs (ex post) to facilitate the orderly resolution of the problems. But they also provide ex ante incentives to market participants. We discuss these issues at the end of Chapter 9.

Chapter 10 is devoted to the analysis of the institutional framework for an efficient implementation of prudential regulation (with both micro- and macro-prudential perspectives) and the execution of resolution policies. Unlike financial regulation, the institutional architecture of financial authorities has not been the subject of much academic interest until recently. We argue in favor of a decentralized institutional framework for identifying systemic risk. We also highlight financial stability committees as coordination frameworks for assessing and executing prudential and resolution policies.

Chapter 8

Justifying prudential regulation

In the wake of the GFC of 2008–2009, the terms systemic risk and macro-prudential regulation came to the forefront. Traditional banking regulation had largely disregarded systemic risk by focusing on individual institutions. This lack of a macro-prudential perspective, which is essential to preserve financial stability, constituted the main shortcoming of prudential regulation before the crisis. The traditional, micro-prudential regulation framework also failed by allowing banks to operate at very low levels of capital and to avoid controls through regulatory arbitrage and through soft supervision of key risks.

Several proposals for public intervention in financial markets have been discussed under the macro-prudential umbrella, including macro-prudential regulation, macro-prudential policies, macro-prudential tools, and macro-prudential authorities. Sometimes, however, the rationale behind the proposals is not entirely clear, nor is the meaning and scope of the terms used. In this chapter, we present a conceptual discussion of the fundamentals supporting public intervention in financial markets to justify whom to regulate and how to do it.

8.1 A conceptual roadmap

A first observation on a conceptual roadmap is that the distinction between micro-prudential and macro-prudential regulation, policies, tools, and authorities is complex and somewhat artificial. Therefore, it is important to have complementary approaches to and views on financial risk.

The micro-prudential perspective on regulation focuses on the failure of individual financial institutions with a partial equilibrium approach. It aims at limiting the frequency and cost of individual failure of financial institutions such as banks (Bhattacharya *et al.*, 1998; Freixas and Rochet, 2008). The macro-prudential approach focuses on systemic risk and considers the kind of general equilibrium spillover effects that were largely disregarded by regulation before the GFC. The preventive role of the macro-prudential approach consists in limiting the likelihood of a financial crisis and its impact on the economy.

Hence, regulation, policies, tools, and the authorities in charge do not need to assume any specific perspective; but they can serve to complement and reinforce both a micro- and a macro-prudential view. In other words, prudential regulation should consider inputs from both the micro-prudential and the macro-prudential approaches to financial risk in order to use policies and calibrate the available instruments and tools with the objective of preserving financial stability.[1] Chapter 9 contains a more extensive discussion of these issues.

Financial stability reflects a range of situations in which the financial system consistently supplies credit intermediation and payment services that are needed in the real economy. Financial stability is also defined in terms of the capacity of the financial system to manage risks and absorb exogenous shocks as well as those generated endogenously by the financial system (Houben *et al.*, 2004; Schinasi, 2004). Financial instability, however, occurs when problems (or concerns about potential problems) within institutions, markets, payments systems, or the financial system in general significantly impair the supply of credit intermediation services, in the sense that they have a substantial impact on the expected path of real economic activity and risk management (see Rosengren, 2011). Allen and Wood (2006) propose a complementary definition of financial stability. They start by defining the characteristics of an episode of financial instability, then define financial stability as a state in which episodes of instability are unlikely to occur.

Understanding that episodes of financial instability can happen because different kinds of risk materialize is crucial to preserve financial stability. Hence, prudential regulation may achieve its preventive role only if all dimensions of financial risk, i.e., the micro-prudential and macro-prudential approaches, are considered and assessed.

---

[1]Throughout this part, we assume a public interest view on regulation whose the objective is to maximize social welfare. An alternative private interest view includes the possibility that interest groups capture the regulatory process (see Stigler, 1971; Barth *et al.*, 2006).

Complementarity of micro-prudential and macro-prudential regulation is consistent with a number of empirical observations. First, in general, macro-prudential policies are variations of micro-prudential policies. For example, the results from a survey by the International Monetary Fund (2011) make it clear that the core instruments and tools of macro-prudential policy are traditional prudential instruments that have been calibrated to deal with systemic risk and extended with a broader financial system approach. Table 8.1 summarizes the policy instruments that are most used in the macro-prudential toolkit. In addition to instruments traditionally used with a micro-prudential perspective (e.g., capital and liquidity regulation), several jurisdictions have also used a few instruments typically considered to belong to other public policies (e.g., foreign exchange measures as well as monetary and fiscal tools) to achieve macro-prudential objectives.

Second, although the global adoption of a macro-prudential approach is recent, its use has a long history in both advanced and emerging market economies. The United States was probably the first country to implement regulation with a macro-prudential perspective in order to control credit growth in aggregate. Over almost a century until the 1990s, the United States used policy instruments with a macro-prudential approach to ease as well as tighten credit conditions over numerous episodes (see Elliott *et al.*, 2013). Similarly, European countries, with the only exception of Western Germany, adopted direct limits on credit expansion from the 1950s toward the end of the 1970s (see Kelber and Monnet, 2014). Emerging market economies also had a great deal of macro-prudential experiences in the wake of their financial crises in the 1990s. Recently, most of these economies have used numerous macro-prudential measures to mitigate the systemic risks caused by excessive capital inflows.[2]

Third, the origin of the term macro-prudential, which denotes a systemic orientation of regulation and supervision linked to the macroeconomy, can be traced back to the late 1970s and early 1980s. For example, by the mid-1980s, the Bank for International Settlements refers to it as a perspective aimed at supporting the safety and soundness of the financial system as a whole, including the payment system (see Clement, 2010).

---

[2]Brunnermeier and Schnabel (2015) provide a complete historical overview of the measures, including those with a macro-prudential perspective, implemented by central banks around the world.

Table 8.1: Macro-prudential instruments and intermediate objectives.

Objective	Instruments
Mitigate and prevent excessive credit growth and leverage	Counter-cyclical capital buffer
	Dynamic provisioning rules
	Sectoral and time-varying capital surcharges
	Leverage ratio
	Loan-to-value, loan-to-income, and debt-to-income caps
Mitigate and prevent excessive mismatches and illiquidity	Liquidity coverage ratio and net stable funding ratio
	Unweighted limits on less stable funding and currency mismatches
	Margin and haircut requirements
Limit direct and indirect exposure concentrations	Large exposure restrictions
	Limits on net open currency positions
	Central counterparty clearing requirements
Limit the systemic impact of misaligned incentives	Systemic capital surcharges
Strengthen the resilience of financial infrastructures	Increased disclosure
	Structural systemic risk buffer

8.2 Challenges to prudential regulation

Implementing prudential regulation in the financial system is complex. First, it entails the challenges of any type of regulatory effort in a market.[3] In general, a rationale for regulating has its origin in instances of market failure. Regulation in such cases is justified by taming an uncontrolled marketplace that fails to produce results in the public interest. Hence, it is important to determine the market failures that justify prudential regulation in the financial market: externalities, information inadequacies, moral hazard, and coordination problems, among others.

Once a rationale for regulating is identified, a first concern is to determine whether to regulate. In answering this question, the market and all its failings should be compared with regulation and all its failings. There are several reasons that regulation is not optimal. For example, it could be that the market, in spite of its failings, provides a superior outcome once the costs of regulation are considered. Financial regulation has direct and indirect costs, including the potential reduction in growth and the possible distortions in the allocation of funds to firms and households, which should be carefully weighed when introducing regulation.

In addition, the introduction of new regulation can have unintended consequences that, in turn, undermine its power. For example, Allen and Gale (2007) argue that one bad regulation (a deposit insurance) does not justify another (capital requirements).[4] Moreover, the threat of regulatory capture and regulatory arbitrage are two phenomena that add costs to the regulatory process, shift risks, and might make regulation ineffectual. The decision on whether to regulate, and the proper design of efficient regulation, should take into account this kind of phenomena and market reactions.

Regulatory capture, i.e., the entity influences its regulator to favor its interests, has been long studied. Its pervasiveness in the financial sector has been well documented (see Woodward, 2000, and the references therein). Boot and Thakor (1993) argue that a clear case of regulatory failure occurs when a regulator fails to appropriately represent the best interests of those it is meant to represent. Recent examples of the willingness of the financial sector to capture the regulatory process are documented by Bloomberg

---

[3]See Baldwin *et al.* (2013) for a complete analysis of the theory and practice of regulation.

[4]However, Allen *et al.* (2015) find that under some conditions the combination of capital regulation and deposit insurance is welfare improving.

(2010): "With power from Congress to oversee the previously unregulated $615 trillion market for over-the-counter derivatives, it [the Commodity Futures Trading Commission] has become one of the hottest lobbying spots in town."

Regulatory arbitrage, i.e., the shifting of business to less regulated markets, is also pervasive in the financial industry. For example, Houston *et al.* (2012) provide empirical, international evidence suggesting that a type of regulatory arbitrage takes place at the international level, where banks transfer funds to markets with looser banking regulations. One of the challenges of regulation is to deal with financial innovation that appears to overcome regulation, e.g., shadow banking. Shadow banking came to the forefront during the global financial crisis. This non-banking, non-regulated sector was indeed doing banking activities. As long as this sector provides deposits, problems in the sector can result in massive deposit withdrawals, which can jeopardize financial stability. Should the shadow banking sector be regulated? To properly answer this question, one should take into account that one of the reasons this sector has grown in the first place was to arbitrate regulations in the banking sector.

Once a market failure has been identified and regulation is deemed necessary, policymakers need to deal with the challenges of regulating financial risks. Risk has been widely defined as the probability that a particular adverse event will occur during a stated period of time. As discussed in Part 2, identifying and assessing risks is no simple matter given the existence of major discontinuities, non-linearities, and rare events (or black swans). Some sources of risk rarely manifest in the same way through history. This fact is particularly relevant in financial markets where risks, rather than being imposed by exogenous factors, are increasingly endogenous in that they are the result of human decisions and actions. Some events are non-repeating risks, where probabilities cannot be estimated and only subjective assessments are available. In particular, systemic risk is hard to quantify but becomes self-evident under casual observation. Moreover, financial innovation can rapidly change both the sources and the impact of risks.

A second concern to the regulation of risks is whether an emphasis should be placed on prudence or on resilience, i.e., lean versus clean. Prudence aims at identifying risks and their sources to anticipate and reduce the production of hazards. A resilience-based strategy, in contrast, assumes a remedial perspective and emphasizes the importance of mitigating the impact of risks that materialize and ensuring that financial systems continue providing core functions even during a major disruption. The regulation of risk involves the adoption of strategies to minimize the production of risks and is also concerned with mitigating the adverse effects in case they materialize. As a matter of fact, different types of risk need a different combination of ex ante intervention in the form of prudential regulation and ex post action through resolution policies. Moreover, it helps prudential regulation to achieve its objectives when it explicitly commits itself to the contingent steps to be taken in case a financial institution needs to be resolved. Hence, preserving financial stability calls for complementing prudential regulation with remedial policies and contingency plans, i.e., with resolution plans.

A third concern with risk regulation is that it is difficult to identify its outcome because it relies on counterfactuals. In an analogy with the theory of testing hypothesis in statistics, this opens the question of whether regulation should err on the side of "rejecting a true hypothesis" and, thereby, potentially under-regulate a risk, or whether regulation should be biased toward accepting false hypotheses and, therefore, to potentially over-regulate. On one hand, prudential regulation might fail to identify the potential systemic risk existing in the economy and miss the building up of a crisis (Type I error). On the other hand, prudential regulation might overestimate systemic risk and implement measures that are not needed (Type II error).

A related challenge is that it is difficult to define a clear-cut accountability arrangement due to the lack of simple indicators that are directly related to financial stability or the risk of a systemic crisis. Moreover, a financial system's safety net is constituted by, at least, the following functions: financial regulation, lender of last resort, deposit insurance, and resolution policies. In practice, these functions are assigned to more than one agency, including central banks, independent supervisors, and deposit insurance corporations. This shared responsibility for the final outcome makes setting a clear accountability arrangement more difficult.

The design of the institutional framework for financial stability, discussed in detail in Chapter 10, is of key importance to overcome the challenges to prudential regulation. An adequate distribution of mandates and powers among the safety net's agencies, as well as setting up appropriate decision-making and accountability arrangements, are crucial to preserve financial stability. The institutional framework should complement and reinforce the effort of individual agencies in identifying and assessing risks from both the micro-prudential and the macro-prudential perspectives. Choosing a proper regulatory path is complicated by the fact that the relevance of risks is likely to be state-dependent, which causes different and conflicting mixes of regulatory responses. Hence, the institutional setting should facilitate the coordination of policies.

8.3   The need for prudential regulation

In an ideal world of frictionless and complete financial markets (i.e., the Arrow and Debreu, 1954, setting), both investors and borrowers would be able to diversify perfectly and obtain optimal risk sharing by using a complete set of assets that are contingent on all possible future states of the world. Thus, there is no role for financial intermediaries nor for financial regulation. But as soon as one considers transaction costs (e.g., indivisibilities and non-convexities in transaction technologies), perfect diversification is no longer feasible and financial intermediaries are needed. Transaction costs can be monetary costs but can also include search costs as well as monitoring, enforcing, and auditing costs. In such a transaction costs approach, financial intermediaries can be seen as coalitions of individual lenders and borrowers exploiting economies of scale and scope in the transaction technology (see Freixas and Rochet, 2008). Specifically, financial intermediaries add value because they can achieve efficiency gains and fulfill individual liquidity needs through the pooling of short-term deposits and the creation of inside money in a fractional reserve system.

The presence of frictions and transaction costs *per se* do not justify prudential regulation in competitive financial markets as long as there is no collective action problem, no bounded-rationality of market participants, or no aggregate risk. Indeed, financial intermediaries offer callable on demand deposits with a sequential-servicing constraint and fractional reserves, which makes them inherently fragile and exposed to runs. However, as long as there are no collective action problems leading to coordination failures, bank runs must be strictly driven by fundamentals. In other words, bank runs are efficient (Gorton, 1985; Chari and Jagannathan, 1988). Hence, demand deposits and the threat of efficient runs are a key component of market discipline, as emphasized by Calomiris and Kahn (1991) and Diamond and Rajan (2000).

In a rational world with transaction costs, public intervention could improve the equilibrium only if it had a comparative advantage over the private sector in reducing transaction costs. Prudential regulation does not have generally such a comparative advantage. Nonetheless, public policy can help financial contracting by reducing transaction costs; for example, it may strengthen the contractual dimension of the enabling environment, something that has characteristics of a public good. In practice, this may be achieved by improving bankruptcy laws to reduce enforcement costs by providing central counterparties for collateral registries and by standardizing behaviors and formats to facilitate contractual relationships. Hence, there is a rationale for market integrity and conduct regulation.

Another form of transaction costs is more fundamental in financial markets: informational asymmetries. For example, a borrower has information, or simply a better capacity to acquire relevant information, that a lender lacks; this borrower is willing to use this advantage to take actions with the lender's money that are not optimal for the latter. These informational asymmetries and principal-agent relationships lead to a set of market failures, which can happen before contracting (adverse selection), at an interim stage (moral hazard: shirking and risk shifting), or at the end of the contract (costly state verification and a form of market power resulting from relationship lending).[5] In turn, failures that are induced by information asymmetry may show up as credit rationing and even as a market breakdown (Akerlof, 1970). Again, financial intermediaries may help to improve the market equilibrium. Leland and Pyle (1977) show that financial intermediaries can use their retained equity to signal their type so that the efficiency problem in the market equilibrium is partially overcome. Diamond (1984) argues that financial intermediaries can exploit economies of scale by acting as delegated monitors aimed at preventing borrowers' opportunistic behavior that result from both moral hazard and costly state verification (see also Hellwig, 1991; Holmstrom and Tirole, 1997).

As in the cases discussed earlier, the role for regulation is then to provide the public goods required to ease the constraints on financial activity and to enhance the enabling environment, this time along the informational dimension. For example, market transparency and corporate governance regulation could facilitate market discipline through the flow, standardization, and reliability of information, as well as through a suitable framework for firms that specialize in assessing and verifying information, e.g., auditors and rating agencies. However, as long as market failures are caused by transaction costs and asymmetric information only, there is no need to regulate financial intermediaries by themselves.

---

[5]The literature on these topics has developed enormously starting from the seminal papers by Akerlof (1970), Stiglitz and Weiss (1981) and Mankiw (1986) on adverse selection, Innes (1990) on moral hazard, Townsend (1979) on costly state verification, and Sharpe (1990) and Rajan (1992) on relationship lending.

A first rationale for prudential regulations emerges if one adds collective action problems to the set of market failures. As shown by Diamond and Dybvig (1983), a financial intermediary could be considered as a coalition of depositors that provides the members with insurance against idiosyncratic liquidity risk, which is privately observed. Moreover, a bank offering demand deposit contracts, investing a fraction of them in long-term investments, and keeping the rest in liquid assets, i.e., a fractional reserve bank, can implement an optimal risk sharing allocation as long as patient depositors do not withdraw early. However, even rational depositors cannot internalize the benefits of acting in a coordinated way because the interaction between depositors has two equilibria: the efficient one and a bank run equilibrium. A coordination failure among depositors, coming from a lack of confidence in their bank, may lead to socially inefficient and self-fulfilling bank runs.

A remedy to prevent rational coordination failures leading to bank runs is to introduce a deposit insurance scheme. In fact, deposit insurance was introduced early on as a response to the bank runs during the Great Depression of the 1930s. While deposit insurance can reestablish the efficient equilibrium, it can also undermine market discipline and promote public moral hazard, with market participants willing to take excessive risk and shift the costs to the deposit insurer. In turn, the funding structure of financial intermediaries can be socially inefficient (excessively short-term) and raise their vulnerability to rollover risk (Brunnermeier and Oehmke, 2013). The tradeoff can be partially balanced by an adequate design of deposit insurance premiums and coverages. However, the deposit insurance premia might not be enough to fully internalize public moral hazard (see Chan *et al.*, 1992; Freixas and Rochet, 1998). An ex ante prudential regulation largely based on capital and liquidity requirements to deposit-taking financial intermediaries would also be required to offset public moral hazard. Capital regulation also promotes risk sharing: capital acts as a buffer to absorb losses and helps in avoiding bankruptcy costs and negative spillover effects on other intermediaries (Gale and Özgür, 2005).

Another coordination failure can occur in the interbank market so that illiquid but still solvent banks are forced to close. In addition to being inefficient, this equilibrium could affect the payment system with negative effects to the economy. Indeed, different financial intermediaries are interconnected through their balance sheets because of direct or indirect cross-exposures. The failure of one of them can, thus, affect the soundness of all the others, thereby interrupting the chain of payments. A lender of last resort, another component of the safety net, has been proposed as a response to this coordination failure. It was the response to the collective action problems leading to the banking crisis of the 19th century.

As in the case of deposit insurance, a lender of last resort policy can also foster public moral hazard. Bagehot (1873) proposed a series of rules, including eligible collateral and penalty rates, that should help to mitigate moral hazard. Still, prudential regulation, in particular liquidity requirements, plays a role in mitigating lender-of-last-resort induced moral hazard and in eliminating the coordination failure that may dry up the interbank market.

Chapter 9

Prudential perspectives

Prudential regulation of a financial system needs to take complementary perspectives to mitigate as many risks as possible. A micro-prudential view focuses on individual institutions and markets. This approach assumes that, if financial institutions are safe and sound individually, then the financial system will be stable. The accords of Basel I and II represent examples of this view applied to banking regulation. Unfortunately, the global financial crisis makes it clear that this approach has limited capacity to control market failures leading to systemic risk. Point in time characteristics of financial systems (e.g., the size and interconnectedness of financial institutions) and dynamic considerations (e.g., procyclicality) generally shape the micro-prudential approach and justify a macro-prudential perspective. We will study these perspectives in Sections 9.1 and 9.2.

One needs to acknowledge that the objective of prudential regulation is to control risk and the occurrence of financial crises but not to prevent the failure of all financial institutions. Even with an optimally designed prudential regulation, some failures still occur. In Section 9.3, we discuss the need and implications of resolution policies that facilitate the orderly resolution of financial institutions.

9.1 Micro-prudential perspective

Under the assumption of a perfectly rational world (as in Chapter 8), prudential regulation has a rationale in correcting the market frictions that lead to inefficient equilibria and in complementing other safety net policies, i.e., deposit insurance and lender of last resort. However, to justify the traditional micro-prudential perspective in Basel I and Basel II, it is necessary to add bounded rationality to the picture.

Bounded rationality refers to the cognitive limitations of market participants to gather and, more fundamentally, to process information. For example, financial customers find it hard to assess financial statements when they are not familiar with accounting terminology. They also find it difficult to understand financial contracts when they lack specific knowledge about legal issues. Moreover, small and non-sophisticated financial customers do not acquire information and the knowledge to understand financial contracts because of (1) the cost of doing so and (2) the fact that they could free ride on the effort exerted by others. Hence, their understanding of complicated financial contracts is imperfect and potentially flawed.

As Akerlof and Shiller (2009) argue, once bounded rationality is recognized, sophisticated market participants have incentives to prey on the non-sophisticated ones. The latter group is then unable to exert control rights appropriately, and the possibility of potential consumer abuse is opened. Increasing market transparency and the availability of information do not alleviate the inefficiency because the non-sophisticated financial customers cannot process information adequately. Moreover, non-sophisticated customers are not able to solve the problem by themselves either. They fail to coordinate in forming a coalition to understand financial statements and monitor sophisticated market participants because of a participation friction: some of them would prefer a free ride on the effort by others who, in turn, do not exert effort from the beginning. Hence, this setting justifies a role for regulation with a micro-prudential, consumer-protection perspective. In practice, the Basel I and II prudential proposals came largely as a response to the excessive risk taking and fraud in the Savings and Loan crisis of the 1980s.

Given bounded rationality and the participation friction of non-sophisticated market participants, a regulator has an important role to play. First, a regulator is presumably more sophisticated than the non-sophisticated participants, albeit not more than the sophisticated ones. Second, a regulator has a natural interest in providing public goods so that the participation friction can be solved.

Following Dewatripont and Tirole (1994), a regulator can represent the small and non-sophisticated market participants (e.g., depositors) by issuing prudential and consumer protection regulation. Micro-prudential regulation can be designed to exactly mimic what the large and sophisticated market participants require from other market participants. In particular, the regulator can act as a delegated monitor that imposes incentive-aligning prudential regulation to sophisticated market participants (e.g., banks), especially in terms of required collateral (i.e., minimum capital adequacy ratios). Banks' shareholders with more skin in the game (i.e., more equity capital) should have lower incentives to take risks (Keeley, 1990). This is a fundamental logic behind Basel I and II capital regulation.

The cornerstone of Basel II is micro-prudential and takes the primary form of minimum capital ratio. Capital regulation is the single pillar in Basel I. Basel II improves it and adds two additional pillars: supervision and market discipline. However, much less attention has been given to these two pillars, to the point that some commentators argue that a rebalancing is needed (see Rochet, 2008).

Given that one rationale of this regulation is to protect small, non-sophisticated financial market participants (mainly bank depositors) and that other complementary policies, such as the deposit insurance, can generate public moral hazard, it seems reasonable to constrain them to commercial, i.e., deposit-taking, banks. This approach conforms with the view that the regulation of financial transactions that are privately negotiated by professionals is unnecessary (Greenspan, 1998). Sophisticated investors can fend for themselves outside the protected commercial bank space and discipline each other without any need for prudential rules imposed from the outside. Hence, in this view, there is no justification to incur regulatory and efficiency costs by extending prudential regulation beyond deposit-taking financial intermediaries.

The micro-prudential perspective in Basel II, although necessary, turns out to be insufficient to prevent the abuse of customers and the profound negative impact of the global financial crisis on society and the economy. In response, among a series of financial reforms, the United States Dodd-Frank Act enacted in 2010 aims to enhance investor protection. Nevertheless, regulation creates a wedge between the regulated and unregulated spheres of the financial sector so that even non-sophisticated customers are encouraged to abandon the regulated sector, thereby undermining consumer protection (de la Torre and Ize, 2010). Additionally, the lack of a complementary macro-prudential approach that reinforces the micro-prudential one helps to explain the depth of the crisis.

The micro-prudential view ignores several market failures from which financial instability arises and, fundamentally, ignores systemic risk. Although it recognizes that financial intermediaries could be exposed to correlated risk and aggregate shocks, these are considered to be a limited, exogenous, and invariant component of the risk environment. The endogeneity in financial dynamics and aggregate risk is largely disregarded.

Instead, the notion of systemic risk is largely limited to the consideration of contagion and domino-type effects through which problems in one financial intermediary could trigger the collapse of others. But the system is shown to be more than the sum of its parts and to have different properties. In turn, this induces a series of fallacies of composition: (1) Ensuring the solvency of each institution on its own is erroneously believed to suffice in order to ensure the soundness of the system as a whole. (2) Every individual institution can draw at the same time on a collectively supplied source of liquidity. (3) Every institution can insure itself against aggregate volatility by contracting insurance with other market participants (Brunnermeier *et al.*, 2009; de la Torre and Ize, 2013). Yet, the micro-prudential perspective is necessary because several aspects of systemic risk can be reduced, in part, by micro-prudential regulation by limiting the probability of individual bank failures, by boosting available buffers to absorb the shocks from failures, and by facilitating a quick and orderly resolution of failing institutions.

In addition to these external failures, micro-prudential regulation also fails in itself by allowing banks to operate at very high levels of leverage. According to Admati and Hellwig (2013), regulators overestimate the cost of banks' equity and, therefore, impose minimum capital requirements that are too low. Many banks were operating with small capital ratios before the GFC, fostering excessive risk taking and leaving many of them with thin buffers to deal with the materialization of the risk that built up in the system. As a result, many banks could not absorb losses and had to be rescued using taxpayer money in an effort to avoid the costs of a disorderly liquidation and disposal of assets.

However, it is not clear whether the regulatory failure can be solved by raising capital requirements without complementary measures aimed at controlling regulatory arbitrage. In practice, banks perceive capital to be an expensive form of financing and take steps to use as little of it as possible. For example, banks followed the strategy of migrating activities outside the regulatory perimeter to the potentially riskier non-bank (or shadow banking) sector in an attempt to reduce the cost of capital. Hence, higher capital requirements in the banking sector might trigger more migration of banking activities, increase the risk on the whole system, and make micro-prudential regulation ineffective (Martin and Parigi, 2013; Plantin, 2014). The design of capital regulation should carefully weigh these forces (Kashyap *et al.*, 2008). For example, regulatory arbitrage could be reduced when risk-based capital regulation is applied in such a way that similar risks face the same capital requirement. It could also help to allow the regulator to change the regulatory perimeter in order to consider all relevant risks regardless of the kind of financial institution generating them.

9.2 Macro-prudential perspective

Market failures and limitations of micro-prudential regulation in dealing with systemic risk justify a macro-prudential perspective on financial regulation. Its main concern is the stability of the entire financial system. Thus the macro-prudential perspective complements the micro-prudential view, which is justified by frictions at the individual level. Systemic risk is the key factor separating the realms of these two perspectives and a necessary (albeit not sufficient) condition for the macro-prudential one. Prudential regulation with a macro-prudential perspective has an intrinsically public good component at an aggregate, systemic level. It intends to overcome market failures, externalities, and other sources of aggregate volatility that generate the endogenous dynamics at the core of systemic risk. Table 9.1, adapted from Borio (2003), shows the comparison between the micro-prudential and the macro-prudential perspectives.

The macro-prudential view seeks to address two specific dimensions of systemic risk: the cross-sectional and the time dimensions (Borio, 2003). The cross-sectional dimension reflects the distribution of risk in the financial system at a given point in time. This approach suggests that the scope of the prudential framework should be rather broad. First, the activities of

Table 9.1: Comparing the micro and macro-prudential perspectives.

	Micro-prudential	Macro-prudential
Rationale	Represent non-sophisticated investors	Promote system-wide stability
Operational objective	Limit distress of individual institutions	Limit inefficient financial crises
Risk model	Exogenous, partial equilibrium	Endogenous (in part), general equilibrium
Prudential control	Individual bank risk	Systemic risk

fund intermediation and risk management are performed, to some extent, by all financial institutions. Although banks are generally more important, other financial institutions also contribute to systemic risk. Second, financial institutions arbitrate regulations by, for instance, migrating activities and the corresponding risks to unregulated areas, i.e., shadow banking. Hence, prudential oversight of the financial system should seriously consider that threats to financial stability may stem from all financial activities, even unregulated ones.

The macro-prudential cross-sectional approach proposes regulatory standards to individual financial institutions according to their contribution to aggregate risk. The measurement of each individual institution's contribution to systemic risk has been a topical issue of academic research in recent years, see Chapters 5 and 6. Multiple dimensions matter in measuring systemic risk contributions. One area of general consensus on measurement relates to the size of institutions: larger institutions have greater system-wide significance. Indeed, a set of financial institutions have been declared as "systemically important" (SIFIs) at both the international and national levels. They are subject to tighter prudential standards, e.g., higher capital requirements, and more frequent and intense supervision. Another area of relative agreement is interconnectedness, which could give rise to contagion, fire sales, and other spillover effects.

The time dimension reflects the procyclicality of the financial system. Along this dimension, the macro-prudential perspective is particularly relevant. First, it considers the endogeneity of risk. Second, controlling procyclicality provides a rationale for building up buffers in upswings so they can be relied upon when rough times arrive. This approach helps reduce systemic risk in two ways. First, it strengthens the resilience of financial institutions to deteriorating macroeconomic conditions because the equity cushions could be better used to absorb losses. Second, the buffers reduce the amplitude of the financial cycle, thereby limiting systemic risk. This "leaning against wind" aspect of the time dimension of systemic risk is particularly important regarding liquidity, an aspect largely forgotten before the global financial crisis.

As with regulation in general, some policies that are undertaken with a macro-prudential rationale can have side effects with unintended consequences, for example, promoting public moral hazard. During a crisis it can be socially optimal to intervene with the aim of speeding up the recovery of financial and real activity, although ex ante it would be also optimal to commit not to intervene. This creates a time consistency problem. Once these aspects are taken into account, there is a rationale for clearly defined resolution policies that complement macro-prudential regulation. In the rest of this chapter, we discuss the details of the cross-sectional and time dimensions of the macro-prudential view of financial regulation, along with resolution policies.

9.2.1 *Cross-sectional dimension*

A rationale for financial regulation with a macro-prudential perspective stems from negative externalities in financial systems. In general, agents do not internalize these externalities on other agents nor on the economy as a whole. Macro-prudential regulation is, then, justified to the extent that the overall costs of market failures (that can lead to a financial crisis) due to these externalities exceed both the private costs of failure and the additional costs of regulation (De Nicolo *et al.*, 2012).

Systemic banking crises are costly. Laeven and Valencia (2013) estimate the median output loss due to crises is 23.2 percent of GDP, while Chang *et al.* (2013) find that suicide rates were 4.2 percentage points higher in Europe and 6.4 percentage points higher in American countries in 2009 than if earlier trends had continued. The high social and economic costs of financial failures can significantly increase the social benefits of bailing out insolvent institutions.

Historically, large insolvent banks are more likely to be bailed out by governments than smaller insolvent banks. For example, during the financial crisis following the collapse of Lehman Brothers, the EU explicitly pledged to support relevant institutions (EU Summit October 12, 2008). Hence, behavioral externalities in the form of herding dynamics can raise the odds that bailouts occur. Financial institutions engaging in risky behavior might expect to be bailed out due to the high costs of policy inaction, and the probability of a bailout increases when they herd. For example, financial intermediaries have an incentive to correlate their risks so that they become "too many to fail," (Acharya and Yorulmazer, 2007; Farhi and Tirole, 2012) to grow bigger to become "too big to fail," or to play key roles in the payment system and the interbank market to be considered "too interconnected to fail."

Collective moral hazard and behavioral externalities introduce a wedge between private and social outcomes, which in turn provides a rationale for macro-prudential regulation aimed at inducing the internalization of externalities. For example, to limit the too-big-to-fail problem, regulation could consider capital surcharges and size limits. Proposals to tame SIFIs include a Pigovian tax that increases with the size of the institution and feeds into systemic risk funds that are empowered to intervene early (Freixas and Rochet, 2012); a capital levy similar to the operation of margin accounts calibrated so that the bank's CDS (Credit Default Swap) spread remains below a certain maximum (Hart and Zingales, 2011); and ring-fencing the systemically important parts of an institution (Independent Commission on Banking, 2011).

Instruments that can be used with the macro-prudential objective of controlling risk taking due to herding dynamics also include discretionary adjustments in regulatory buffers and transaction-oriented norms, for example, caps on debt-to-income and loan-to-value ratios. Collective moral hazard concerns can also be attenuated via requirements on systemically important financial institutions to hold minimum levels of debt that are subject to some form of haircut in the event of failure, e.g., contingent convertible bonds. Yet, ex post intervention cannot be completely ruled out. Hence, it is important to improve crisis management and resolution schemes (see Section 9.3). In recent years, as a response to the global financial crisis, regulations have requested so-called living wills to be drawn up by SIFIs. A living will denotes a contingency plan of a financial institution in case it becomes insolvent and needs to be resolved. Proposals to induce the internalization of externalities that are rooted in the too-many-to-fail problem includes the punishment of the worst performers (Farhi and Tirole, 2012) and the ex ante commitment to apply penalties to shareholders as part of the resolution process (Ponce, 2010).

Externalities also come from the interconnected nature of the financial sector business, especially the banking sector. Externalities can be channeled through the payment system, as discussed by Freixas and Parigi (1998); the interbank market (see Allen and Gale, 2000; Rochet and Tirole, 1996); and the international financial markets (Kodres and Pritsker, 2002). But there are more subtle, and nonetheless material, propagation mechanisms. Cifuentes *et al.* (2005) discuss contagion effects through intermediaries' exposure to similar assets. Wagner (2011) analyzes the interconnectedness and contagion effects that result from mutual hedging and diversification. Bebchuk and Goldstein (2011) show that self-fulfilling lending freezes by financial intermediaries can occur when the firms they lend to are interconnected. The vulnerability of the financial system to contagion effects depends on the geometry and complexity of the networks. Interconnectedness can dramatically exacerbate the non-linearities resulting from aggregate shocks, amplifying their impact in turbulent times. Again, to the extent that financial intermediaries do not take into account their actions' effects on the risk of other institutions and the financial system as a whole, interconnectedness externalities can lead to financial instabilities by excessively exposing the financial system to shocks and contagion.

Aggregate risk together with interconnectedness externalities can lead to a gradual build-up of systemic risk during booms (Adrian and Shin, 2010) that causes financial gridlock, serial institutional failures, and sharp contraction of liquidity and hedging possibilities during the bust. Even if bank managers are aware of the risks, the strategic complementarity of their actions makes it difficult for them to internalize the externalities. The declaration of the former Citigroup chief Charles Prince to the *Financial Times* in 2007 is a good example: "When the music stops, in terms of liquidity, things will be complicated. But as long as the music is playing, you have got to get up and dance. We are still dancing." In other words, it does not pay for an individual institution to leave if others stay, although it is better for all to coordinate if they can collectively stop. During a bust, as asset prices decline, the impact of one intermediary's withdrawal (e.g., indirectly by failing to roll over existing commitments or directly by defaulting) is transmitted to others, and the associated flights to liquidity are exacerbated by interconnectedness. In turn, asset prices continue falling due to fire sales by intermediaries in an attempt to find liquidity. Moreover, funding and market illiquidity reinforce each other, leading to vicious liquidity spirals that multiply the initial shocks (Brunnermeier and Pedersen, 2009).

Similarly, behavioral externalities justify ex ante macro-prudential regulation, as well as ex post resolution policies if a crisis occurs. The threats of contagion-triggered failures have been considered by the micro-prudential view of financial regulation. However, the global financial crisis highlights the fact that interconnectedness has to be dealt with in more targeted ways. It is important that intermediaries internalize their impact on the soundness of the system as a whole. To this end, it is crucial to measure the contribution of each institution to systemic risk. Such measures could enable the application of systemic capital surcharges that are proportional to the institution's contribution to systemic risk. In this context, it is necessary to develop causal measures of systemic risk.[1]

---

[1] For practical reasons, most of the risk measures described in Chapter 6, e.g., those by Acharya *et al.* (2012) and Adrian and Brunnermeier (2016), identify tail correlations in one way or another, but they are not causal.

Depending on the systemic importance of an institution on the network, it is also worth considering liquidity rules that encourage holding liquid assets and penalize short-term wholesale funding. In certain financial transactions, such as those with derivatives, a central counterparty clearing house backed by large prudential buffers can reduce the counterparty risk of over-the-counter markets (Duffie and Zhu, 2011). Yet, the remaining externalities and network vulnerabilities in financial systems are important, so more extreme proposals have also been envisaged. For example, interconnectedness externalities can provide a rationale for a Volcker type rule where commercial and investment banking functions are clearly separated. As discussed previously, the benefits of introducing these regulations need to be weighed against the potential efficiency costs and the possibility that intermediaries rapidly arbitrate regulations.

Another externality in the cross-sectional dimension has to do with information and free riding. Information has characteristics of a public good, so it might be under-provided by the market. If information gathering is costly, then the impossibility of intermediaries to privately appropriate its benefits (because others will free ride on the information gathered) implies that the value of information will not be properly internalized. As a result, it can be privately optimal for financial intermediaries (as well as other private sector providers of information, for example, auditors, rating agencies, and other analysts) to stop gathering information before reaching the socially optimal level.

Moreover, free riding has other systemic consequences in addition to the under-provision of information. For example, intermediaries might make their decisions purely on the basis of what they infer from the signals issued by other agents that are taking actions confronted with similar choices; or they might use the same risk models simply because they have become the norm in the industry. This kind of decision-making process leads to financial instability because the collective behavior is characterized by the replication by some intermediaries of what others are doing. In this setting, systemic risk could increase after good news, and even a small piece of unexpected information can lead to financial instability because, simply, all agents react similarly to news. For example, this may explain why the failure of Lehman Brothers in the United States triggered a market freeze with devastating systemic consequences. It is also useful to understand the strong growth of structured financial products before the crisis and the lack of interest in the aftermath.

A policy response to the under-provision of information by market participants is to produce systemic-oriented information. In recent years, the number of jurisdictions that regularly publish financial stability reports (with analysis and research from a systemic perspective) has increased strongly. One of the objectives of financial stability reports is to spread useful information for market participants to internalize externalities and to correct potentially risky market developments. According to Born *et al.* (2014), these reports are successful in curbing dangerous developments in financial markets. Even more important, however, speeches and interviews by senior regulators are more effective to reassure markets and coordinate a resolution once problems have erupted.

Other policy responses focus on the governance and compensation schemes of private sector providers of information. For example, the bad performance of the major rating agencies regarding structured finance products is suggested to be at the heart of the subprime crisis. The big Icelandic banks that failed in 2008 were awarded AAA ratings by Moody's Investors Service in 2007; and Enron Corporation was rated investment grade by the major rating agencies just four days before it declared bankruptcy in 2001. These examples suggest that the rating agencies became more permissive in giving ratings at the same time that they were changing their pricing model from an investor-pays to an issuer-pays one (Ponce, 2012).

9.2.2 *Time dimension*

The consideration of aggregate shocks can give rise to aggregate endogenous risk and lead to persistent, amplified, and unstable macro-financial dynamics with major real output consequences. In particular, general equilibrium effects, the endogeneity of risk, the procyclicality of financial variables, and the leverage of financial intermediaries acquire major importance when considering aggregate shocks. Again, market failures and externalities justify regulation with a macro-prudential perspective across the time dimension of systemic risk.

Due to financial frictions, the materialization of aggregate risks have persistent effects on real economic variables, e.g., activity and employment, because the financial condition of firms are negatively affected and its recomposition takes time. As a consequence of an adverse aggregate shock, borrowing firms suffer a loss in their net worth, which in turn reduces the value of the collateral they can offer in order to borrow. Over time, firms use retained earnings to rebuild their capital. Hence, the reduction in aggregate spending has a lasting impact on activity (Bernanke and Gertler, 1989). An alternative explanation for the persistent effects of aggregate shocks is that financial constraints force fire sales during a bust; in turn, assets become less productive as they are allocated to less skilled entrepreneurs (Lorenzoni, 2008; Korinek and Davila, 2017).

The dynamic of asset prices implies that these negative effects can be amplified. Bernanke *et al.* (1999) argue that the original shock is magnified due to the endogenous default of borrowers, which further reduces the price of capital and collateral. Hence, leverage plays a central role. Leveraged firms might fire sale assets as a reaction to an aggregate shock. In this case, Kiyotaki and Moore (1997) find that a loss spiral in asset prices can occur, which further erodes the borrowing capacity of firms and amplifies the negative effects. This is particularly important when the firms are banks. In a downturn, falling asset prices erode banks' capital, forcing deleveraging and adding to the downward spiraling of asset prices.

Leveraging procyclicality also plays a major role. Adrian and Shin (2009), and Adrian *et al.* (2012) argue that the increase of asset prices in an upturn boosts banks' capital through valuation adjustments. This procyclical increase in capital raises the leveraging capacity of banks and the supply of credit, which raises asset prices further. Leveraging procyclicality can also be a consequence of herding dynamics induced by reputational concerns (Rajan, 1994, 2006). An asset manager may take excessive risk when all other asset managers behave similarly. (Remember our quotation of Charles Prince: "... as long as the music is playing, you have got to get up and dance.") If things turn out well, managers make profits. If things go badly but losses are systemic and affect everybody, managers are evaluated leniently by the market and by their stockholders. This kind of dynamic paves the way to increasing systemic risk, with potentially large social costs.

Turning the focus to liquidity, a wedge between individual and social values of liquidity can occur because of non-internalized pecuniary externalities. In this case, intermediaries that face the same aggregate shocks and respond to similar incentives do not internalize the system-wide implications of their individual actions. They find themselves borrowing too much at short maturities because they undervalue the impact on systemic risk of such funding structure (Cao and Illing, 2010; Perotti and Suarez, 2011). Some banks prefer to free ride on the liquidity provision due to their limited liability. In times of systemic stress, the resulting gap between aggregate demand and liquidity supply exacerbates the vulnerability of the financial system and leads to downward asset price spirals.

Liquidity procyclicality can also have important consequences to the real sector when aggregate risk materializes (see He and Krishnamurthy, 2011; Brunnermeier and Sannikov, 2014). In practice, financial intermediaries hold liquidity buffers that allow them to absorb relatively small shocks. As long as this is the case, risk remains largely exogenous and without macro-financial consequences. However, risk becomes endogenous when an aggregate shock makes financing constraints to become binding. The endogenous component of risk plays a major role in magnifying the impact of the original materialization of aggregate risk. An example is the fire sale of assets by leveraged agents. As in the case of capital, liquidity procyclicality in the upturn makes the financial system highly vulnerable to aggregate risk. Indeed, in good times, exogenous risk decreases, inducing financial intermediaries to lever up and hold lower precautionary liquidity buffers.

It is interesting to observe that despite the presence of sophisticated short-term creditors, market discipline is not effective to prevent procyclicality. Moreover, wholesale funding can foster procyclicality. Huang and Ratnovski (2011) find that in upturns where intermediaries are taking excessive risk, sophisticated investors are better off staying than disciplining the intermediary. If the upturn continues, short-term creditors benefit from the upside. As soon as the downturn starts, they control losses by exiting early. Wholesale creditors can do so because smaller and non-sophisticated investors are protected by deposit insurance schemes, so that they have no reason to run. This is a clear example of public moral hazard induced by deposit insurance regulation. It calls for an appropriately designed pricing of deposit insurance and for other regulation that seriously considers the time dimension of systemic risk.

Aggregate risk, together with participation frictions and public moral hazard, dynamically alters principal-agent incentives. Therefore, it seems apparent that regulation should also respond dynamically to align incentives to the social interest. The failure of regulation to dynamically calibrate instruments and coordinate policies as required by the phase of the financial cycle can lead to a systemic crisis because the persistence and amplification effects combine with herding behavior by financial intermediaries. For example, imagine that a financial innovation, e.g., securitization of structured products, causes a credit boom and that regulation fails to raise prudential requirements in response to it. In this case, banks have much to gain in taking excessive risk, which amplifies the initial shock, adds to systemic risk, and might lead them to fail at the same time. This observation, together with international interconnectedness, helps to explain why problems in the relatively small subprime mortgage market in the United States spread all over the world as a global financial crisis in 2008.

Empirical evidence suggests that excessive credit growth is a good early warning indicator of systemic crises (see Drehmann and Juselius, 2014, and the references therein). Interestingly, however, the peculiarities of the Basel II prudential regulation do not deter further excessive risk-taking incentives; instead the regulation could boost these because the risk measurement underlying the weighting of assets in the risk-adjusted capital requirement is procyclical (Repullo *et al.*, 2014; Repullo and Suarez, 2012). Dewatripont and Tirole (2012) conclude that the Basel I and II policy of ignoring macroeconomic shocks in the determination of capital adequacy requirements leads to too much intervention in recessions and too much leniency in booms. Moreover, the appropriate calibration of capital requirements after a negative aggregate shock also has important consequences. Indeed, one of the functions of bank capital is to serve as a buffer to absorb unexpected losses. If regulation does not allow this buffering function, e.g., by not allowing the release of extra capital buffers after a negative aggregate shock, banks attempting to fulfill capital regulation further contract the credit supply. In this case, a credit crunch can occur. In fact, Dewatripont and Tirole (2012) find that lowering capital adequacy requirements during a recession (in conflict with Basel rules) does a better job at isolating banks from macroeconomic shocks. (But it also creates sizable incentives for gambling by under-capitalized banks.)

As financial crises correlate with economic cycles, prudential regulation needs to be responsive to aggregate shocks in an attempt to reduce procyclicality. This provides a rationale for a dynamic alignment of the macro-prudential perspective to financial regulation, which is indeed at the core of the Basel III proposals (de la Torre and Ize, 2013). According to Dewatripont and Tirole (2012), optimal regulation requires that macroeconomic shocks be automatically neutralized to keep the incentives of the investor in control unchanged. In practice, this neutralization can take the form of dynamic provisioning or a (Basel III) counter-cyclical capital buffer. These tools introduce rules intended to control procyclicality by increasing regulatory requirements in upturns and relaxing them during downturns.

Counter-cyclical capital buffers have been envisaged to deal with predictable boom-bust dynamics in the credit market. Repullo and Suarez (2012) find that there is scope for them as long as banks are sufficiently capitalized through a preservation buffer (an extra capital requirement introduced by Basel III on top of the minimum capital requirement). This requirement allows the use of the counter-cyclical buffer during downturns. Several jurisdictions are implementing different versions of counter-cyclical capital buffers.

Most of them follow a rule-based approach for buffering, although the scope of application can vary from specific sectors (e.g., mortgages in Switzerland) to all the credit activities of the banking sector. Often this approach is implemented through indicator variables. The indicator variables that trigger buffering can differ across jurisdictions; but usually they are selected according to their capacity to identify the endogenous formation of systemic risk. Generally, a measure of the credit cycle (e.g., credit growth and credit-to-GDP gap) is included in the set of indicator variables. The experience with counter-cyclical capital buffers is limited, particularly with respect to their release. To date, only the United Kingdom has released a counter-cyclical capital buffer of 0.5% as a reaction to *Brexit*, the June 23, 2016 referendum that approves the exit of United Kingdom from the European Union.

Even before counter-cyclical capital buffers were proposed in Basel III, Spain and several Latin American countries had introduced counter-cyclical (also called dynamic) provision schemes for loan losses. The traditional loan loss provision system consists in anticipating the expected losses due to non-repayment of loans and accounting them in the balance sheets of banks as a reduction to the loan's face value. At maturity, if the loan is repaid, the provision is released; but if the loan is not (fully) repaid, the provision covers (part of) the losses. Through counter-cyclical provisioning a fund is accumulated in periods when the expected losses are lower than those in the long-run (through-the-cycle) level. Counter-cyclical provisions are not released in periods with low default rates, but they are used to cover losses in a downturn. For the case of Spain, Jimenez *et al.* (2017) find that dynamic provisioning smooths credit supply cycles and, in bad times, supports firm performance. In a formal model, Gomez and Ponce (2015) study the effectiveness of counter-cyclical capital buffers and dynamic provisioning to provide the correct incentives to bank managers; they conclude that both of them are adequate policy tools.

It is important to notice that rule-based macro-prudential regulation (as most implementations of counter-cyclical capital buffers and dynamic provisioning) serve adequately well when confronting predictable dynamics. However, regulation could still need to deal with the materialization of large and unpredictable risks. If this is the case, a macro-focused, state-contingent, or even discretionary oversight are needed (de la Torre and Ize, 2013).

Regarding liquidity, Cao and Illing (2010) conclude that imposing equity requirements as a buffer are inferior mechanisms for coping with systemic liquidity risk, which instead requires a combination of liquidity regulation ex ante and lender of last resort policy ex post. In particular, liquidity regulation should include a mix of Pigouvian taxation on short-term funding and quantitative regulation that imposes a constraint on the portfolio share that financial intermediaries invest in short-term assets (Farhi *et al.*, 2009; Perotti and Suarez, 2011). In other words, this calls for systemic liquidity requirements that penalize short-term wholesale funding.

As part of the Basel III revisions, two minimum standards for liquidity are introduced: the liquidity coverage ratio and the net stable funding ratio. The liquidity coverage ratio requires banks to maintain high-quality liquid assets at least equal to their projected net cash outflows over a stressful 30-day period. The net stable funding ratio requires banks to have available stable funding (i.e., the portion of capital and liabilities expected to be reliable over a one-year horizon) at least equal to required stable funding, which is measured based on the broad characteristics of the liquidity risk profile of an institution's assets and off-balance-sheet exposures. The intent of these ratios is to constrain banks' ability to take liquidity and maturity risk in a manner similar to the way capital adequacy regulations limit banks' ability to take solvency risk. As with capital regulations, banks faced with binding limits on their liquidity ratios are likely to respond along all the possible margins, including holding a relatively larger proportion of liquid assets and obtaining longer maturity funding. However, liquidity regulations are also likely to be similar to the capital adequacy regulations in that, over time, banks will find ways of complying with the letter of the regulation while getting around its intent, i.e., regulatory arbitrage.

9.3   Resolution policies

During the global financial crisis of 2008–2009, traditional, micro-prudential banking regulation failed because of unforeseen spillovers and externalities that were disregarded while their monitoring was essential to preserve financial stability. The incorporation of the macro-prudential perspective to regulation aims to fill this gap. To prevent the materialization of sufficiently large and low-probability aggregate shocks from overwhelming the buffering capacity of the system, it is tempting to set prudential buffers high enough to totally eliminate systemic risk. But this action can be socially too costly; it seems socially optimal to experience a financial crisis in some extreme states of nature. If this is the case, then ex post interventions aimed at speeding the recovery of financial and real activity are justified. These interventions include the resolution and reallocation of the good assets of failing financial intermediaries, the recapitalization or bail out with public funds of some of them in an attempt to stop the most calamitous effects of the crisis, and the provision of aggregate liquidity via a lender of last resort policy or an accommodative monetary policy. Crisis management and resolution policies are complementary to macro-prudential regulation. Proper, clear-cut, and well-defined resolution policies facilitate the macro-prudential task and, therefore, limit political interference by strengthening market discipline and reducing the need for regulatory interventions.

Resolving failed banks through standard insolvency proceedings is difficult because of the special characteristics of their financial structure, their particular role in the functioning of financial markets and the economy, and the considerable social costs and externalities imposed by bank failures. Thus, special bank resolution regimes are set with the objective of minimizing the associated costs. Costs include the disruptions to the failed bank's customers, the potential contagion to other intermediaries, the fiscal costs that can arise from payments through a deposit insurance fund or direct recapitalization, and the negative effects of rescues on bankers' incentives.

Public authorities use various resolution methods, ranging from purely private solutions to the use of public funds and monetary policy. Private-sector resolution techniques include mergers and acquisitions, in which a bank experiencing difficulties can be acquired by a healthy bank, and purchase and assumption, in which the failing institution enters receivership, its charter is terminated and all or part of its assets and liabilities are transferred to another institution. Sometimes, a purchase and assumption resolution plan includes some public guarantees in order to facilitate the process. Yet, it could be the case that a permanent solution cannot be immediately implemented. In this case, a bridge bank is set up to maintain banking operations until reaching a permanent solution. Another possibility is to split a failing bank in two. A "good bank" retains the performing assets while a "bad bank" receives the remaining assets to be restructured or liquidated. A final solution is closure, liquidation of the bank's assets and deposit payoff, which includes the use of deposit insurance funds. White and Yorulmazer (2014) conclude that private-sector resolution is a preferred option in terms of minimizing costs associated with bank failures, although it may not be a feasible option when the failing institution is large and complex or when its failure occurs during a systemic crisis.

Ex post public assistance to undercapitalized intermediaries is likely to have first-order social benefits (Mailath and Mester, 1994), particularly after a large aggregate shock materializes (Ponce, 2010), and especially if intermediaries are systemically important ones (Ponce and Rennert, 2015). In this case, a bail-out policy (e.g., government-led asset purchases, quantitative easing or targeted recapitalization programs) are called for. During a crisis, the private sector might be unable to spontaneously perform the necessary recapitalization of the system because of incremental risk aversion or because the investment costs incurred by individual investors exceed the returns that each one could appropriate. However, collective returns would exceed collective costs if all private parties coordinate the rescue. Hence, public intervention could improve the coordination failure because of its ability to provide public goods and its comparative advantage in absorbing and spreading risk. These capabilities of the public sector hinge on its power to enforce taxation. Thus, fiscal capacity is very important to allow bail-out policies. On the contrary, a weak fiscal situation could amplify financial instability through a loop channeled through public debt unsustainability (Caballero and Farhi, 2013).

In a systemic crisis, aggregate liquidity shortages arise (1) if firms with excess liquidity cannot lend to firms with liquidity gaps as in Woodford (1990); (2) if the interbank market closes down because of a coordination failure of market participants as in Freixas *et al.* (2000, 2004) and Rochet and Vives (2004); or (3) if all intermediaries find themselves on the demand side of the market as in Holmstrom and Tirole (1998). In any of these cases, public intervention is justified because it can improve the post-crisis equilibrium due to its advantage in solving coordination failures and providing public goods. Typically, a lender of last resort policy allows banks to offer their illiquid assets as collateral in exchange for getting access to liquidity. Hence, a lender of last resort policy provides a mechanism for preventing widespread bank failures. Indeed, bank clearinghouses in the United States mitigated this risk up to the 1907 banking crisis, when banks became less willing to provide this service. This fact provides one of the primary reasons for the creation of the Federal Reserve (Bordo and Wheelock, 2013).

However, the ex post intervention by a lender of last resort can undermine ex ante incentives and market discipline. Banks are likely to become relatively more illiquid if there is a lender of last resort to provide funding during crisis times. Moreover, prior to lender of last resort policies, bank runs had been the primary way of forcing severely under-capitalized banks into resolution. The best-known guidance for the provision of emergency liquidity assistance by a lender of last resort is from Bagehot (1873): to lend freely on good collateral but only to solvent intermediaries at a penalty rate. However, banks still have incentives to take more risks if they believe that the lender of last resort will lend to some insolvent banks, a belief validated by the increasing difficulties in assessing solvency problems and distinguishing them from liquidity problems in the midst of a crisis.

Brunnermeier and Sannikov (2014) argue that in times of crisis, a countercyclical monetary policy can be welfare improving. Looser monetary policy in the midst of a financial crisis gives windfall capital gains to financial intermediaries because their assets are of longer duration than their liabilities. Moreover, Farhi and Tirole (2012) find that an accommodative monetary policy is preferable because those intermediaries with the better assets, i.e., the most solvent ones benefit most, so this crisis policy is better than others in targeting.

Both accommodative monetary policy and the bail-out of insolvent intermediaries, although ex post socially optimal, can foster ex ante moral hazard. In turn, they could increase the likelihood of large aggregate shocks and systemic crisis. When anticipated, monetary or fiscal support is equivalent to a put option provided to intermediaries free of charge. This option has a social cost that is not being paid by intermediaries. Thus, they may take more risk and hold less liquidity than would be socially desirable. Hence, standard moral hazard analysis suggests that shareholders should be penalized if these resolution policies favor their intermediaries. For example, moral hazard concerns can be attenuated by requiring shareholders to hold minimum levels of debt that can be subject to some form of haircut or dilution in the event of failure, e.g., contingent convertible bonds (CoCos, see Calomiris and Herring, 2013, and the references therein) or by committing to demote bank managers and other stakeholders as in Ponce (2010).

Effective crisis management and resolution policies require strong coordination among regulatory, monetary, and fiscal policies. Private resolution methods may be preferred for idiosyncratic failures but impossible to apply during a systemic crisis. In this situation, resolution is more challenging since it entails tradeoffs between disruptions arising from a disorderly liquidation and the fiscal costs and moral hazard resulting from using public funds for recapitalization. Hence, a state-contingent resolution strategy with strong coordination among public authorities is needed. Moreover, such coordination is also required ex ante in order to complement and reinforce policies with the prudential objective of preserving financial stability. This is the topic of Chapter 10.

Chapter 10

Institutional frameworks for financial stability

The implementation of prudential regulation and the execution of resolution policies face important institutional challenges. Basically, it implies a delegation of power to specific regulatory authorities. Delegation opens a series of principal-agent problems because the interests of a regulator (an agent) may not coincide with those of society (the principal). Hence, a clear specification of the agency's mandates and tools, as well as correctly designed governance and accountability arrangements, are necessary to align incentives. The optimal design of the contract between society and regulators matters because it determines responsibilities, powers, constraints, and compensations. Also important is the architecture and institutional design of the safety net because it specifies the ways in which synergy among agencies must be exploited, as well as how checks and balances must operate.

The consideration of systemic risk, financial stability concerns, and a macro-prudential perspective to financial regulation adds complexity to the institutional challenges.

First, systemic risk is multidimensional and dynamic, so that rarely the information, capacity, resources, and expertise of a single authority (e.g., micro-prudential regulator, deposit insurance corporation, central bank) are enough to identify and assess threats to financial stability in a timely way. If one opts for a single regulator, central banks are in a better position than other agencies because of their responsibilities with monetary policy their role in the payment systems.

Second, the outcome in terms of financial stability generally does not depend on action by a single authority but on the combined actions by the multiple agencies involved in the financial safety net, i.e., regulators and deposit insurers, and even on the actions of macroeconomic authorities conducting monetary and fiscal policies. These agencies can have conflicting views and support policies that damage the efficiency of the other agencies' policies, thus paving the way toward financial instability. For example, asset prices tend to increase in the case of low interest rates, which can trigger excessive leverage and lead to price boom-bust spirals. Hence, the challenge to designing a strong institutional framework for financial stability is to provide the means for the agencies to make explicit their conflicting views and to act in a coordinated manner. In turn, coordination should help regulatory agencies to internalize the potential side effects of their actions on financial stability. Among other things, this coordination implies a clear division of tasks and responsibilities in which all involved agencies receive incentives to control systemic risk, including the mandate to preserve financial stability.

Third, it is challenging to define clear-cut accountability arrangements because of the multi-agency nature of the task of ensuring financial stability and the difficulty of identifying the results of prudential regulation, which in general relies on speculation regarding counterfactuals. However, an optimal design of the financial stability framework should take into account these particularities in order to improve accountability. For example, Boyer and Ponce (2012) show that using two supervisors instead of just a single one to assess different dimensions of risk (e.g., idiosyncratic and systemic) would be welfare improving because the principal could use the information provided by one of them to assess the performance of the other. In turn, this architecture improves transparency and accountability so that the threat of regulatory capture diminishes and costs to society are lower.

10.1   Financial stability committees

An effective institutional response to develop a strong framework for financial stability seems to be the creation of financial stability committees. These bodies have gained momentum since the global financial crisis, albeit each with specific features and particularities. (More than 30 countries have created committees since 2009.)

The actual implementation differs from one jurisdiction to another, possibly to account for differences in their financial systems, the existing regulatory arrangements, and legal and institutional constraints; however, it is possible to identify key principles guiding their design. First, financial stability committees serve as a means of sharing information and views on a regular basis among the financial safety net agencies, i.e. to coordinate systemic risk identification and assessment. In turn, this helps to complement and reinforce the micro- and the macro-prudential perspectives to financial stability (Bergara *et al.*, 2014); see Section 10.3. Second, financial stability committees also coordinate prudential and resolution policies (see Section 10.4). In general, prudential policy coordination is achieved by issuing recommendations to constituent agencies, while direct regulatory actions and the responsibility for their outcome continues to lie with these agencies. Accountability is facilitated by effective systemic risk identification and measurement, together with coordinated policy and the responsibilities of constituent agencies.

In the United States, the 2010 Dodd-Frank Wall Street Reform and Consumer Protection Act established a new Financial Stability Oversight Council chaired by the U.S. Treasury. Council members are the federal and state regulators; securities supervisors, including the Federal Deposit Insurance Corporation; and an independent insurance expert appointed by the President. The Council has a clear statutory mandate that creates, for the first time, a collective responsibility for identifying systemic risks and responding to emerging threats to financial stability. It operates under a committee structure to promote shared responsibility among the member agencies and to leverage the expertise that already exists at each agency. The Council forms committees around its various statutory responsibilities and core issues that relate closely to risks in which more than one agency has a significant interest. Additionally, to help with the identification of emerging risks to financial stability, it can provide direction to, and request data and analyses from, the newly created Office of Financial Research housed within the Treasury. The Council issues recommendations to constituent agencies and plays a coordinating role, while direct regulatory and supervisory authority remains with the constituent agencies.

In the UK, the Financial Policy Committee became active on April 1, 2013, under the 2012 Financial Services Act. The Committee's primary role is to identify, monitor, and take action to remove or reduce risks that threaten the resilience of the UK financial system as a whole. One way that the Committee can mitigate threats to resilience is by raising awareness of systemic risks among financial regulators and other market participants. Under the Financial Services Act, two other agencies were established: the Prudential Regulation Authority and the Financial Conduct Authority. The Prudential Regulation Authority, a subsidiary of the Bank of England that replaces the former Financial Services Authority, is responsible for the regulation and supervision of most systemic institutions (including non-banks). The Financial Conduct Authority, a separate institution not overseen by the Bank of England, is responsible for regulating other financial firms, for ensuring the relevant markets function well, and for the regulating the conduct of all financial firms. The Financial Policy Committee can issue directions and recommendations to the Prudential Regulation Authority and Financial Conduct Authority. The regulators are required to act as soon as reasonably practical. If a regulator decides not to implement a recommendation, it must explain the reasons for not doing so (which is called a "comply or explain" basis). The Committee can also make recommendations regarding financial stability to other bodies, though not on a comply or explain basis.

Following the recommendations by de Larosiere Group (2009), the European Union started amending its supervisory architecture in January 2011 with the creation of three new European Supervisory Authorities (for banks; for securities and markets; for insurance and pensions). These new agencies have limited powers and resources, with ultimate decisions remaining at the national level. Under the Single Supervisory Mechanism that became fully operational in 2014, however, broad supervisory powers were formally conferred to the European Central Bank regarding all credit institutions in the European Union but, fundamentally, only those declared systemically important. A newly created European Systemic Risk Board is responsible for the macro-prudential oversight of the EU financial system and the prevention and mitigation of systemic risk. In pursuit of its mandate, the Board monitors and assesses systemic risks and, when appropriate, issues non-binding warnings and recommendations through a "comply or explain" mechanism. Members with voting rights in the Board include the president and vice-president of the European Central Bank, the chairpersons of the three European Supervisory Authorities, the governors of national central banks of the member states, one member of the European Commission, and representatives of the Advisory Scientific Committee and the Advisory Technical Committee. These two advisory committees conduct research to inform decisions by the Board, and provide advice and assistance on issues relevant to identifying and assessing systemic risk.

Other countries where the effects of the global financial crisis were less severe have also improved the institutional organization of their financial stability nets along similar conceptual lines. For example, in August 2013, the Swedish government announced its new, strengthened framework for financial stability, clarified the roles and responsibilities of the relevant authorities, and created a Financial Stability Council. For efficiency and accountability reasons, main responsibilities for prudential regulation (with both micro-prudential and macro-prudential approaches) and control of policy instruments were assigned to a single Financial Services Authority. The Financial Stability Council serves as a forum for discussion among the government, the prudential regulator (the Riksbank, the central bank), and the National Debt Office (which acts as bank resolution authority) about financial stability and any needed actions. The exchange of information and coordination in the Council helps constituent agencies on their duties. Each authority, however, is responsible for decisions within its area of responsibility.

Several countries in Latin America have also strengthened their institutional framework for financial stability. For example, Uruguay established in 2011 a Financial Stability Committee, which shares all the key characteristics of the Swedish one. In this case, the central bank plays a key role in the coordination of stability mandates, owing to its expertise, credibility, and independence. In many other countries, e.g., Chile and Mexico, it is the Ministry of Finance that has the lead because of its role in the budget and legislative process. Nevertheless, the central bank generally has an important role in advising and leading the analytical work.

The conceptual organization and governance of financial stability committees slightly differ across countries. These differences relate to existing (pre-crisis) arrangements, different tradeoffs with other policies, different degrees of development of financial systems, as well as legal constraints. Nevertheless, their rationale seems to be the same: to share information and views about evolving systemic risks, to develop identification, assessment and monitoring tools, to coordinate mitigating policies, and to enhance accountability of decision-making authorities. These issues are analyzed in the remaining sections of this chapter.

10.2 Challenges to the institutional design

The institutional design of a strong and efficient framework for financial stability should guarantee that systemic risks are identified timely and measured correctly. It should also facilitate the coordination of prudential and resolution policies. Moreover, the institutional framework should solve principal-agent frictions through enhanced transparency and accountability, and keep the implementation costs as low as possible. Hence, the architecture of the institutional framework should incentivize the best-suited agency to act, or foster the combined and coordinated actions of several of them if this is the most efficient response. Incentives are very important because financial stability can require prompt, unpopular, and politically sensitive actions that, combined with the accompanying uncertainty, could bias an agency toward inaction.

Effective, timely identification and measurement of systemic risk requires weighing Type-I against Type-II errors. The former are associated with failing to identify the potential risks in the economy and miss the building up of a crisis; Type-II errors result from intervening when it is not required, with the associated direct costs of a potential reduction in growth and the possible distortions in the allocation of funds to firms and households. To guarantee that financial stability net's agencies can act appropriately, their access to relevant information is crucial.

Central banks have a natural leading role in gathering useful information because their activities are at the core of financial systems; central banks are responsible for the soundness of payment systems and, often, for financial supervision. Moreover, central banks have technical capacity and independence, reputation, and a systemic view because of their role in monetary policy. However, the sources of systemic risk are multidimensional, and the information that a single agency accesses could allow only a partial, incomplete evaluation of the real situation. Moreover, potentially dangerous developments might not be under the spotlight of any agency because its scarce resources are applied to fulfill more immediate or direct mandates. For example, internal risk models of banks working in isolation and using traditionally micro-prudential stress tests might not adequately identify bubbles or measure systemic risk. A simple model in Section 10.3 shows that setting a coordinated architecture in a committee for identifying and measuring systemic risk not only reduces the associated direct costs, but also increases the likelihood of correctly identifying threats to financial stability. Fischer (2017) argues that committees can aggregate a large volume of diverse information about current and expected future economic conditions. This information includes anecdotes and impressions gleaned from business and other contacts, which can provide insights that are not recorded in current data releases.

If it is operational, active, and effective, a prudential policy with a macro-prudential approach cannot ignore other policies in place, nor can these policies ignore the existence of a macro-prudential approach to financial regulation. This challenge is formally analyzed in Section 10.4. As we highlighted in Chapter 8, it is essential to coordinate resolution policies for macro-prudential regulation. Having in place clear-cut, well-defined resolution policies facilitates the macro-prudential task by strengthening market discipline and limiting the political interference, as the mechanisms of resolution are then non-negotiable. We also highlighted the importance of micro-prudential regulation in complementing the macro-prudential one. Several aspects of systemic risk can be reduced, in part, through micro-prudential regulation that limits the probability of individual bank failures and boosts available buffers to absorb losses.

To create a strong and stable financial system, the relationship of (micro and macro) prudential policies with monetary and fiscal policies must be also considered. The ideal situation is the one in which prudential policy targets the sources of threats to financial stability while monetary policy remains focused on price stability. At the same time, however, side effects from one policy to another can reduce effectiveness in achieving either policy's objectives. This is why coordination is important; the trend prior to the global financial crisis of separating financial regulation from central banks should be reversed. Moreover, macro-prudential policy may be not enough to ensure financial stability, so other policies have to play their part in complementary areas, which also calls for policy coordination.

When monetary policy affects banks' risk-taking, the separation of monetary policy from banking regulation could be inefficient (Agur and Demertzis, 2012). Monetary easing relaxes financial constraints (asset prices rise and borrowers' net worth increases), lowers the external finance costs, and eases credit conditions. Asset prices have a tendency to increase when interest rates are low, which can trigger excessive leverage and lead to price booms. Monetary tightening can lower borrowers' capacity to repay debts and cause collateral constraints to bind, which could lead to adverse asset price externalities and financial instability. Roldan-Pena *et al.* (2016) show that including financial stability considerations as an additional objective of monetary policy indeed reduces the volatility of financial variables.

Theoretical literature suggests that monetary and macro-prudential policies are complements rather than substitutes. The strengthening of the banking system's resilience reduces the side effects of implementing a restrictive monetary policy. Macro-prudential tools can provide buffers in order to process unexpected shocks, thus lessening the risk that monetary policy will run into a lower bound on interest rates (International Monetary Fund, 2013a). As long as the objectives are output and price stability, the literature typically concludes that the optimal solution is to use both monetary and macro-prudential policies. For example, a heterodox monetary policy based on tightening reserve requirements, which induces banks to lengthen the maturity of their funding, helps internalize the adverse systemic implications of short-term wholesale funding (Kashyap and Stein, 2012). Indeed, as documented by Federico *et al.* (2013, 2014), developing countries have extensively used reserve requirements as a substitute for counter-cyclical, interest rate-based monetary policy because the latter has been constrained by concerns with the exchange rate and carry trade after the global financial crisis.

The institutional design challenge is to provide a field for macro-prudential and monetary policy coordination without distorting incentives and accountability. The interaction among banking market conditions, monetary policy decisions, and bank risk-taking further favor the centralization of macro-prudential responsibilities within the monetary authority (Blanchard *et al.*, 2010). Central banks provide liquidity, which is crucial for financial stability. They also understand financial markets, institutions, and infrastructure, understanding that is necessary for macro-prudential regulation. Clearly, financial stability affects economic activity and price stability. However, financial stability mandates to central banks should be compatible with monetary policy responsibilities. Centralization of powers would increase the risk of the central bank taking a soft stance against inflation and lead to a loss of credibility and reputation. Moreover, central banks would have a more complex mandate when they are also responsible for macro-prudential regulation, making accountability more difficult. In practice, it seems there is no "one size fits all" across the world because arrangements range from a complete consolidation of prudential regulation inside central banks to separation of supervisory responsibilities to independent agencies. Nevertheless, central banks have financial stability as an intrinsic objective. Before the GFC, two out of three central banks received an explicit mandate for financial stability. This proportion rose to four out of five after the crisis. Similar figures are obtained if only those central banks with no supervisory mandate are considered (see the Ingves, 2011, Report). Moreover, the mandate is implicit in most of the rest; around 90 percent of the central banks surveyed recognize their role on financial stability.

Financial stability can be strongly affected by macroeconomic imbalances because macroeconomic shocks can spill over to the financial system and jeopardize stability. Hence, the macroeconomic situation matters, and an appropriate fiscal policy is important to minimizing the potential for macroeconomic shocks. Moreover, a strong fiscal policy is necessary to provide the safety of sovereign debt and to avoid adverse feedback loops between sovereign debt and the financial system (International Monetary Fund, 2013b). Bailouts and other resolution policies often require the use of taxpayers money, so the fiscal situation matters for rapid stabilization after a major stability problem occurs.

Another important rationale for the need of coordination between fiscal policy and macro-prudential regulation is that the latter is unlikely to be effective in curbing certain dynamics without complementary prudent fiscal policy. For example, not taxing mortgage rents provides a relief of mortgage interest rates in a way that encourages households to borrow. Since high mortgage debt can make households more vulnerable to shocks, raising taxes on mortgages could complement macro-prudential tools, e.g., loan-to-value and debt-to-income regulation, to control risk exposures. In practice, finance ministries have assumed a key, explicit role regarding financial stability by chairing most of the financial stability committees created since the global financial crisis.

10.3   Systemic risk identification and assessment

In this section, we deal with the problem of organizing the institutional architecture for identifying and assessing systemic risk. We start with a simple example to highlight the basic tradeoffs and evaluate the relative performance of centralizing the assessment in a single agency versus decentralizing in more than one. Then we introduce a more complete model in order to derive sufficient conditions under which a coordinated institutional arrangement (a committee) for identifying systemic risk outperforms a framework characterized by a single macro-prudential authority. The analysis is inspired by Sah and Stiglitz (1986).

10.3.1   *A decentralized framework for identification*

The problem for prudential authorities is to determine which financial institutions in the system should be declared systemically important because their contributions to systemic risk are high enough. In practice, prudential authorities do not observe directly the systemic risk contributions. Instead, they observe information that, though correlated with the financial institution's true contribution to systemic risk, is only an imperfect signal of it. For example, variables such as size and interconnectedness are generally used for systemic risk assessment.

To capture these ideas in a simple way, we denote by r the contribution to systemic risk of a financial institution and assume that prudential authorities own an imperfect technology to identify and measure systemic risk. This technology assigns an institution to the systemically important category with a probability $0 \leq p(r) \leq 1$. This probability is increasing in the true systemic risk contribution r of the financial institution being assessed. Note that a financial institution with sufficiently high systemic risk contribution may not be declared systemically important because of the imperfection of the supervisory technology. Using the systemic risk technology entails a fixed, direct assessment cost a each time it is applied.

In what follows, we highlight the basic tradeoffs that result from the imperfection of the technology to assess systemic risk. We then discuss how the tradeoffs could be balanced by an optimally designed institutional arrangement for identifying systemically important financial institutions.

We consider two forms of organizing macro-prudential surveillance between two prudential authorities leading to centralized and decentralized assessment of systemic risk. In the *centralized* structure, each financial institution is first evaluated by a prudential authority (e.g., a micro-prudential supervisor); those deemed to be systemic by this authority are forwarded to another authority (e.g., a macro-prudential authority or the central bank). In this centralized institutional arrangement, a financial institution is declared systemically important only by the last prudential authority assessing its riskiness. In the *decentralized* structure, prudential authorities assess financial institutions independently. If one authority does not declare a financial institution as systemically important, then the other one performs an independent assessment of the same institution. In this decentralized arrangement, a financial institution may be declared systemically important separately by each of the two prudential authorities.

The probability that a financial institution will be declared systemically important in the institutional arrangement I is denoted by $q^I(r)$, where the superscripts $I = C$ and $I = D$ represent the centralized and the decentralized arrangements, respectively. The total ex ante (expected) cost of assessing systemic risk is denoted by A^I. The probability of declaring a financial institution as systemically important and the associated systemic risk assessment cost under centralized and decentralized arrangements are as follows.

Centralization. In this case, the financial institution is first assessed by one prudential authority, which must deem it systemically important and forward the file to the other authority, with probability $p(r)$. The probability that the latter authority finds the same institution to be systemically important is again $p(r)$. Hence, the probability that a financial institution will be declared systemically important under a centralized arrangement is $q^C(r) = p^2(r)$. Regarding the assessment cost, the first authority always assesses the financial institution, while the second one does so only with probability $p(r)$ (i.e., if the first authority forwarded the institution for assessment to the second prudential authority). Hence, the assessment cost is $A^C = a(1 + p(r))$.

Decentralization. In this case, the probability that the financial institution that is assessed by the first authority will be declared systemically important is $p(r)$. When it is not declared to be of systemic importance, which happens with probability $1 - p(r)$, the same institution is assessed by the second authority, which will declare it as systemically important with probability $p(r)$. Hence, the probability that a financial institution will be declared systemically important is $q^D(r) = p(r)(2 - p(r))$. The assessment cost is $A^D = a(2 - p(r))$.

Comparisons. Considering only the direct assessment costs, decentralization is cheaper than centralization. The (relative) assessment costs per financial institution that is declared systemically important are

$$\frac{A^C}{q^C(r)} = \frac{c(1 + p(r))}{p^2(r)}, \text{ and } \frac{A^D}{q^D(r)} = \frac{c}{p(r)}$$

under a centralized and a decentralized institutional arrangement, respectively. Direct inspection reveals that the former is more costly than the latter.

More importantly, the probability that a financial institution will be declared systemically important is higher under a decentralized than under a centralized institutional arrangement: $q^D(r) - q^C(r) = 2p(r)(1 - p(r)) \geq 0$. To see the intuition behind this result, consider a hypothetical situation in which there is only one prudential authority. The probability of declaring a financial institution systemically important would then be the same in the two systems, namely $p(r)$. Since the second authority in a decentralized arrangement declares at least some other financial institutions as systemically important and the second authority in a centralized arrangement does not declare some others, the actual proportion of financial institutions declared systemically important in a decentralized arrangement must exceed that in a centralized one.

The imperfection of the technology being used by prudential authorities to assess systemic risk implies errors in identifying systemically important financial institutions. In analogy from classical theory of statistical inference, we think of a Type-I error when a financial institution that should be declared systemically important is not, while a Type-II error occurs when a financial institution is declared as systemically important but should not.

Given the imperfection of the supervisory technology (and then the systemic risk assessment errors in each single use of it), the structure of the institutional arrangement for systemic risk identification alters the relative incidence of each type of error. In order to analyze the relative performance of centralization versus decentralization, remember that a decentralized institutional arrangement declares as systemically important a larger proportion of financial institutions compared to a centralized arrangement. Hence, the incidence of Type-I error is relatively higher in a centralized arrangement, whereas the incidence of Type-II error is relatively higher in a decentralized one.

Therefore, if it is more important for policymakers to avoid Type-I errors, i.e., if it is more important to identify most of the truly systemically important financial institutions, then decentralization outperforms centralization. Moreover, decentralization entails lower relative assessment costs than a centralized arrangement. However, if it is more important to avoid Type-II errors, then a centralized institutional arrangement performs better than a decentralized one, although relative assessment costs are higher. Given the systemic risk profile of a financial system and the effectiveness of the supervisory technology, the optimal institutional arrangement for systemic risk identification will depend on the policymakers' solution to these tradeoffs.

10.3.2   *Coordinated assessment in a committee*

We have seen that prudential authorities receive a binary, although imperfect, signal concerning the contribution to systemic risk of each financial institution. In practice, authorities receive a much richer set of signals. Most of the time, these signals not only are imperfect but they are also noisy, so that authorities have to decide under what conditions to declare a financial institution as systemically important. Moreover, the structure of the institutional arrangement influences this decision.

We now enrich the basic model by assuming that prudential authorities observe a signal $s = r + \theta$ about a financial institution under consideration, where θ has density function $s(\theta)$ and cumulative distribution function $S(\theta)$, which is independent of the distribution of r. Given the noise (θ), prudential authorities set a threshold value $\underline{s}$ such that if $s \geq \underline{s}$, then the financial institution is declared as systemically important. Hence, each authority assigns a financial institution to the systemically important category with probability $p(r, \underline{s}) = 1 - S(\underline{s} - r)$.

The design of the institutional arrangement for assessing systemic risk affects the optimal threshold $\underline{s}$. Moreover, in addition to centralization and decentralization of systemic risk identification tasks, this extended setup allows the consideration of a third arrangement, *coordination*, in which decisions are made to optimize the combined output of the two prudential authorities.

While the previous subsection looked at fixed r, here we study all realizations r. We assume that the objective function of prudential authorities is maximizing the expected value of the identified systemic risk. We denote by $f^I(r)$, $I = C, D$ and (for simplicity) by $p(r)$ the probability density of a financial institution to be classified as systemically important. Then, the goal is to maximize $E(r \times f(r))$.

Under centralization, the second authority chooses $\underline{s}^C$ in order to maximize $E(r \times p^2)$. First-order conditions for an interior maximum are $E(r \times p \times \frac{\partial p}{\partial s}) = 0$. Under decentralization, authority $i = 1, 2$ sets the threshold value $\underline{s}^D$ in order to maximize $E(r \times p_i \times (2 - p_j))$, where $j = 1, 2$ with $j \neq i$. Focusing on the symmetric Nash optimum, the corresponding threshold value is characterized by $E(r \times (2 - p_j) \times \frac{\partial p_i}{\partial s}) = 0$. Under coordination, the threshold value $\underline{s}^{CO}$ is set to maximize the combined output of the two authorities: $E(r \times p_i \times (2 - p_j)) + E(r \times p_j \times (2 - p_i))$, so that it is obtained by equating $E(r \times (1 - p) \times \frac{\partial p}{\partial s})$ to zero.

It is not hard to prove that $\underline{s}^{CO} > \underline{s}^D > \underline{s}^C$. (See Sah and Stiglitz, 1986, for a formal proof.)) That is, systemic risk assessment is more conservative under decentralization than under centralization, but it is less conservative than under coordination.

This result shows how the organization of the institutional arrangement influences systemic risk assessment:

1. Under *centralization*, the first authority knows that its assessment will be rechecked by the second authority. Moreover, the latter knows that all risk profiles it assesses were previously assessed by the first authority.

2. Under *decentralization* each authority knows that its assessment of a financial institution as systemically important will not be cross-checked; it also knows that the set of risk profiles it is examining includes many that have already been examined elsewhere but not declared systemically important. Hence, prudential authorities are more conservative than in a centralized institutional arrangement, i.e., require a larger threshold value to assign a financial institution to the systemically important category.

3. Under *coordination*, authorities act more conservatively than under uncoordinated decentralization. This is because, in a decentralized institutional arrangement, authorities do not take into account the negative externality they exert on one another as much as they do when their threshold values would be coordinated. More precisely, when declaring some financial institution as systemically important, an authority reduces the potential of the other authority to find a systemically important financial institution; so by acting coordinately they are more conservative.

Comparing the performance of the three institutional arrangements (centralization, decentralization and coordination) is more difficult than in the simple example that we presented. That is because the threshold values are set differently in the different systems, so the Type-I and Type-II errors are different. However, it is possible to derive a set of sufficient conditions under which one system performs better than the others. Let us assume that under decentralization, an authority chooses its threshold level such that the number of financial institutions declared systemically important is the same as that chosen optimally under centralization. Of course, this is not optimal. However, if decentralization performs better than centralization with this non-optimal threshold, then it surely will do even better with the optimally chosen threshold value. Moreover, since a coordinated system considers the external effects that one prudential authority poses on the other, it performs better when threshold values are optimally chosen. Following analogously the analysis in Sah and Stiglitz (1986), it is possible to show that decentralization outperforms centralization if the aggregate screening function is more discriminating for the former. This is true if the screening is very tight. In this case, a committee outperforms decentralization, which in turn outperforms centralization.

Interestingly, the condition under which a committee outperforms other arrangements for risk assessment, i.e., very tight screening, occurs more frequently when risk is systemic. In particular, screening is very tight in the tail of the distribution. In this case, the threshold values of the authorities are high, meaning that it is more demanding to declare a financial institution as a systemically important one. Otherwise stated, financial stability committees outperform other arrangements for systemic risk assessment in situations in which authorities want to correctly assign those systemic institutions to the systemically important category.

10.4 Prudential policy coordination

We now turn to analyzing the implementation of prudential policy. As discussed before, incumbent agencies may have different opinions regarding the course of required action. For example, a situation could arise in which the central bank wants to ease monetary policy because of its concern with activity, while a prudential regulator prefers to keep interest rates high because lowering them can trigger excessive leverage and lead to asset price booms. It is important to make opposing interests explicit in order to achieve the best outcomes for society.

There are two common mechanisms for achieving a decision about the policy to be implemented. The first involves explicit communication and negotiation in a committee. The second, by contrast, depends on a unilateral decision by one of the authorities, which is then followed by the others. These two mechanisms are compared in a simple model. The results allow us to conclude that the committee is more likely to achieve coordination and that, although the committee is slower, it outperforms unilateral policy implementation even when rapid decision making matters.

Consider a situation in which one of two incompatible prudential policies, A or B, must be implemented. The interesting case is the one in which the two prudential authorities in charge of making a decision have opposite views regarding the policy to be implemented. Let us assume that the central bank prefers policy A, and the prudential regulator prefers policy B. However, the agencies each prefer to adopt its less preferred policy rather than to be incompatible, i.e., both authorities value successful coordination. Hence, there is the following preference order for the central bank. First, the central bank is best off if both itself and the prudential regulator choose A; second, both of them choose B; third, it chooses A and the prudential regulator chooses B; and in the worst case, it chooses B and the prudential regulator chooses A. Assume the prudential regulator has a similar order of preferences provided that its preferred policy is B.

If the institutional arrangement is a committee, both agencies meet (possibly many times before a maximum number of meetings, N, is reached) to agree on a joint action. In each meeting, either agency can insist on following its preferred policy or concede to follow the other agency's preferred policy. Under the alternative decision-making mechanism, in each period, either agency can implement its preferred action or wait to the next period. We denote the value of using one's preferred policy by a, and the additional value of successful coordination by c. Table 10.1 shows the payoffs of both

Table 10.1: Coordination game with $n \leq N$ periods remaining.

Central bank	Prudential regulator	
	Concede/Wait	Insist/Do B
Insist/Do A	$a + c, c$	z, z
Concede/Wait	w, w	$c, a + c$

prudential authorities in any period, n.[1] The payoffs w and z vary according to the institutional arrangement and the number of period remaining, n. These payoffs are endogenous continuation values. In particular, under a committee arrangement with n periods remaining, if both agencies insist on their preferred policies, then they will meet again and, thus, z is the expected payoff of the repeated game with $n - 1$ periods remaining. If decisions are made individually and each agency does its preferred action, then z is equal to a and w is the expected continuation value of the game with $n - 1$ periods remaining because both authorities have postponed their decision to the following periods.

In this setting, Farrell and Saloner (1988) prove that with a finite fixed horizon, the committee structure unambiguously outperforms unilateral decision making provided that the value of successful coordination, c, is large enough. As highlighted before, the value of coordinated prudential policy seems to be larger on systemic risk matters when negative policy externalities are important. Hence, even though the committee is less likely to reach an outcome before the deadline (i.e., before N meetings), if it does, the outcome is certainly coordinated. This implies that a committee arrangement should be preferred as a coordination device for prudential policy aimed at containing systemic risk.

Although the committee does better when there is no value attached to the speed of decision making, it is slower. And speed is often important regarding the prudential regulation of systemic risk. Important private and social costs can materialize because of regulatory forbearance that derives, for example, from a systemic financial crisis. One might expect, therefore, that allowing for an important discount for every period in which no coordination is attained might reverse the conclusion that the committee structure is better. However, this is not the case. The committee system

---

[1]Readers familiar with game theory will recognize a modified version of the "battle of the sexes" game in this structure of payoffs.

gives unambiguously better payoffs in equilibrium. Intuitively, the greater speed of the unilateral policy-making system is outweighed by the fact that the committee causes fewer errors through a better coordinated prudential policy.

Effective identification and assessment of systemic risk, as well as strong coordination among regulatory, monetary, fiscal, and resolution policies, are necessary to preserve financial stability. Formal analysis suggests that an effective institutional response in order to develop a strong framework for financial stability consists of the creation of financial stability committees. These committees serve as a device for sharing information and views among the financial safety net authorities. In turn, this sharing helps to complement and reinforce the micro- and the macro-prudential perspectives, outperforming other arrangements for systemic risk identification and assessment. Moreover, the coordination in the conduct of prudential policies that is achieved by committees also outperforms the outcome of other institutional arrangements. Hence, the recent global trend to establish financial stability committees to control systemic risk and preserve financial stability seems to be supported by formal analysis. In practice, whether financial stability committees effectively serve their purpose of keeping financial systems in a range of stability is still an empirical question.

Bibliography

Acemoglu, D., Ozdaglar, A., and Tahbaz-Salehi, A. (2015). Systemic risk and stability in financial networks, *American Economic Review* **105**, 2, pp. 564–608.

Acharya, V. (2009). A theory of systemic risk and design of prudential bank regulation, *Journal of Financial Stability* **5**, pp. 224–255.

Acharya, V., Cooley, T., Richardson, M., and Walter, I. (2011). Market failures and regulatory failures: Lessons from past and present financial crises, Asian Development Bank Institute 264.

Acharya, V., Engle, R., and Richardson, M. (2012). Capital shortfall: A new approach to ranking and regulating systemic risks, *American Economic Review Papers and Proceedings* **102**, pp. 59–64.

Acharya, V., Pedersen, L., Philippon, T., and Richardson, M. (2017). Measuring systemic risk, *Review of Financial Studies* **30**, pp. 2–47.

Acharya, V. and Yorulmazer, T. (2007). Too many to fail — an analysis of time-inconsistency in bank closure policies, *Journal of Financial Intermediation* **16**, 1, pp. 1–31.

Admati, A. and Hellwig, M. (2013). *The Bankers' New Clothes: What's Wrong with Banking and What to Do about It* (Princeton University Press).

Adrian, T. and Brunnermeier, M. (2016). CoVaR, *American Economic Review* **106**, pp. 1705–1741.

Adrian, T., Colla, P., and Shin, H. (2012). Which financial frictions? Parsing the evidence from the financial crisis of 2007-9, NBER Working Paper No. 18335.

Adrian, T. and Shin, H. (2009). Money, liquidity, and monetary policy, FRB of New York Staff Report No. 360.

Adrian, T. and Shin, H. S. (2010). Liquidity and leverage, *Journal of Financial Intermediation* **19**, 3, pp. 418–437.

Agenor, P.-R., Miller, M., Vines, D., and Weber, A. (1999). *The Asian Financial Crisis - Causes, Contagion and Consequences* (Cambridge University Press, Cambridge).

Aglietta, M. (1996). Financial market failures and systemic risk, CPPI Working Paper 1996-01.

Agur, I. and Demertzis, M. (2012). Excessive bank risk taking and monetary policy, European Central Bank Working Paper No. 1457.

Ahnert, T. and Georg, C.-P. (2018). Information contagion and systemic risk, *Journal of Financial Stability* **35**, pp. 159–171.

Akerlof, G. (1970). The market for lemons: Quality uncertainty and the market mechanism, *The Quarterly Journal of Economics* **84**, 3, pp. 488–500.

Akerlof, G. and Shiller, R. (2009). *Animal Spirits: How Human Psychology Drives the Economy, and Why It Matters for Global Capitalism* (Princeton University Press).

Aliber, R. and Zoega, G. (2014). *Preludes to the Icelandic Financial Crisis* (Palgrave Macmillan, New York).

Allen, F. and Babus, A. (2009). Networks in finance, in P. Kleindorfer and Y. Wind (eds.), *The Network Challenge*, chap. 21 (Pearson Education), pp. 367–382.

Allen, F., Babus, A., and Carletti, E. (2012a). Asset commonality, debt maturity and systemic risk, *Journal of Financial Economics* **104**, pp. 519–534.

Allen, F., Carletti, E., and Marquez, R. (2015). Deposits and bank capital structure, *Journal of Financial Economics* **118**, 15, pp. 601–619.

Allen, F. and Gale, D. (2000). Financial contagion, *Journal of Political Economy* **108**, 1, pp. 1–33.

Allen, F. and Gale, D. (2007). *Understanding financial crises* (OUP Oxford).

Allen, L., Bali, T. G., and Tang, Y. (2012b). Does systemic risk in the financial sector predict future economic downturns, *Review of Financial Studies* **25**, pp. 3000–3036.

Allen, W. and Wood, G. (2006). Defining and achieving financial stability, *Journal of Financial Stability* **2**, 2, pp. 152–172.

Anand, A. and Schwarcz, S. (2016). Systemic financial risk: Can new regulations protect the public from widespread economic failure? Wilson Center Canada Institute 18.

Ariff, M. and Khalid, A. (2000). *Liberalization, Growth and the Asian Financial Crisis* (Edward Elgar, Cheltenham).

Arrow, K. and Debreu, G. (1954). Existence of an equilibrium for a competitive economy, *Econometrica* **22**, 3.

Athanasoglou, P., Georgiou, E., and Staikouras, C. (2008). Assessing output and productivity growth in the banking industry, Bank of Greece Working Paper No. 92.

Augustin, P., Boustanifar, H., Breckenfelder, J., and Schnitzler, J. (2016). Sovereign to corporate risk spillovers, ECB Working Paper No. 1878.

Baba, N. and Hisada, T. (2002). Japan's financial system: Its perspective and the authorities' roles in redesigning and administering the system, *Monetary and Economic Studies* **20**, pp. 43–93.

Bagehot, W. (1873). *Lombard Street: A Description of the Money Market* (London: Henry S. King and Co.).

Baker, A., Hudson, D., and Woodward, R. (2005). *Governing financial globalization: International political economy and multi-level governance* (Routledge, London).

Baldwin, R., Cave, M., and Lodge, M. (2013). *Understanding Regulation: Theory, Strategy, and Practice*, 2nd edn. (Oxford University Press).

Ball, L. M. (2018). *The Fed and Lehman Brothers: Setting the Record Straight on a Financial Disaster*, Studies in Macroeconomic History (Cambridge University Press).

Balla, E., Ergen, I., and Migueis, M. (2014). Tail dependence and indicators of systemic risk for large US depositories, *Journal of Financial Stability* **5**, pp. 195–209.

Bank for International Settlements (1994). 64th Annual Report, Bank for International Settlements.

Barandiarian, E. and Hernandez, L. (1999). Origins and resolution of a banking crisis: Chile 1982-86, The Central Bank of Chile.

Barth, J., Caprio, G., and Levine, R. (2006). *Rethinking bank regulation: Till angels govern* (Cambridge University Press).

Bartram, S., Brown, G., and Hund, J. (2007). Estimating systemic risk in the international financial system, *Journal of Financial Economics* **86**, pp. 835–869.

BCBS (2014). The G-SIB assessment methodology - score calculation, Basel Committee on Banking Supervision (BIS).

Bebchuk, L. and Goldstein, I. (2011). Self-fulfilling credit market freezes, *The Review of Financial Studies* **24**, 11, pp. 3519–3555.

Benoit, S., Colletaz, G., Hurlin, C., and Perignon, C. (2013). A theoretical and empirical comparison of systemic risk measures, Working Paper, HEC Paris.

Benoit, S., Hurlin, C., and Perignon, C. (2017). Pitfalls in systemic-risk scoring, Working Paper, HEC Paris.

Bergara, M., Licandro, G., and Ponce, J. (2014). *Challenges to Financial Stability — Perspective, Models and Policies (Volume II Towards Financial Stability — Macroprudential Policy and Perspectives)*, chap. Financial Stability Committees: An Institutional Response to New Challenges (ASERS Publishing), pp. 9–22.

Bernanke, B. and Gertler, M. (1989). Agency costs, net worth, and business fluctuations, *The American Economic Review* **79**, 1, pp. 14–31.

Bernanke, B., Gertler, M., and Gilchrist, S. (1999). The financial accelerator in a quantitative business cycle framework, in J. Taylor and M. Woodford (eds.), *Handbook of Macroeconomics*, chap. 21 (Elsevier), pp. 1341–1393.

Bhattacharya, S., Boot, A., and Thakor, A. (1998). The economics of bank regulation, *Journal of Money, Credit and Banking* **30**, 4, pp. 745–770.

Billio, M., Getmansky, M., Lo, A. W., and Pelizzon, L. (2012). Econometric measures of connectedness and systemic risk in the finance and insurance sectors, *Journal of Financial Economics* **104**, pp. 535–559.

Bisias, D., Flood, M., Lo, A. W., and Valavanis, S. (2012). A survey of systemic risk analytics, *Annual Review of Financial Economics* **4**, pp. 255–296.

Blanchard, O., Dell'Arriccia, G., and Mauro, P. (2010). Rethinking macroeconomic policy, *Journal of Money, Credit and Banking* **42**, 1, pp. 199–2015.

Blass, A. and Grossman, R. (1996). Financial fraud and banking stability: The Israel bank crisis of 1983 and trial of 1990, *International Review of Law and Economics* **16**, pp. 461–472.

Blass, A. and Grossman, R. (2001). Assessing damages: The 1983 Israeli bank shares crisis, *Contemporary Economic Policy* **19**, pp. 49–58.

Bloomberg (2010). Wall Street lobbyists besiege CFTC to shape derivatives rules, Bloomberg news.

Boot, A. and Thakor, A. (1993). Self-interested bank regulation, *American Economic Review* **83**, 2, pp. 206–2012.

Bordo, M. (1990). The lender of last resort: Alternative views and historical experience, *Federal Reserve Bank of Richmond Economic Review* **76**, pp. 18–29.

Bordo, M., Mizrach, B., and Schwartz, A. (1995). Real versus pseudo-international systemic risk: Some lessons from history, NBER Working Paper No. 5371.

Bordo, M. and Wheelock, D. (2013). *The Origins, History, and Future of the Federal Reserve: A Return to Jekyll Island*, chap. The Promise and Performance of the Federal Reserve as Lender of Last Resort 1914–1933 (Cambridge University Press), pp. 59–98.

Borio, C. (2003). Towards a macroprudential framework for financial supervision and regulation? BIS Working Papers No. 128.

Borio, C. and Lowe, P. (2002). Asset prices, financial and monetary stability: Exploring the nexus, BIS Working Papers 114, Bank for International Settlements.

Born, B., Ehrmann, M., and Fratzscher, M. (2014). Central bank communication on financial stability, *The Economic Journal* **124**, 577, pp. 701–734.

Boyer, P. and Ponce, J. (2012). Regulatory capture and banking supervision reform, *Journal of Financial Stability* **8**, 3, pp. 206–217.

Brook, P. (2000). Financial safety nets: Lessons from Chile, *The World Bank Research Observer* **15**, 1, pp. 69–84.

Brownlees, C., Chabot, B., Ghysels, E., and Kurz, C. (2015). Backtesting systemic risk measures during historical bank runs, Federal Reserve Bank of Chicago Working Paper WP 2015-09.

Brownlees, C. and Engle, R. (2016). SRISK: A conditional capital shortfall measure of systemic risk, *Review of Financial Studies* **30**, pp. 48–79.

Brunnermeier, M., Crockett, A., Goodhart, C., Persaud, A., and Shin, H. (2009). *The fundamental principles of financial regulation* (International Center for Monetary and Banking Studies Centre for Economic Policy Research, Geneva London).

Brunnermeier, M., Gorton, G., and Krishnamurthy, A. (2012). Risk topography, NBER Macroeconomics Annual 2011.

Brunnermeier, M. and Oehmke, M. (2012). Bubbles, financial crises, and systemic risk, NBER Working Paper No. 18398.

Brunnermeier, M. and Oehmke, M. (2013). The maturity rat race, *Journal of Finance* **68**, 2, pp. 483–521.

Brunnermeier, M. and Pedersen, L. (2009). Market liquidity and funding liquidity, *Review of Financial Studies* **22**, 6, pp. 2201–2238.

Brunnermeier, M., Rother, S., and Schnabel, I. (2017). Asset price bubbles and systemic risk, CEPR Discussion Paper No. 12362.

Brunnermeier, M. and Sannikov, Y. (2014). A Macroeconomic Model with a Financial Sector, *American Economic Review* **104**, 2, pp. 379–421.

Brunnermeier, M. and Schnabel, I. (2015). Bubbles and central banks: Historical perspectives, CEPR Discussion Paper No. DP10528.

Brunnermeier, M. and Schnabel, I. (2016). *Central Banks at a Crossroads - What Can We Learn from History?*, chap. Bubbles and Central Banks: Historical Perspectives (Cambridge University Press), pp. 493–562.

Bullard, J. (2008). Worry less about systemic risk, more about inflation, The Regional Economist Federal Reserve Bank of St. Louis.

Caballero, R. and Farhi, E. (2013). A model of the safe asset mechanism (SAM): Safety traps and economic policy, NBER Working Paper No. 18737.

Cai, J., Eidam, F., Saunders, A., and Steffen, S. (2018). Syndication, interconnectedness, and systemic risk, *Journal of Financial Stability* **34**, pp. 105–120.

Calomiris, C. and Herring, R. (2013). How to design a contingent convertible debt requirement that helps solve our too-big-to-fail problem, *Journal of Applied Corporate Finance* **25**, 2, pp. 39–62.

Calomiris, C. and Kahn, C. (1991). The role of demandable debt in structuring optimal banking arrangements, *The American Economic Review* **81**, 3, pp. 497–513.

Calvo, G., Izquierdo, A., and Talvi, E. (2003). Sudden stops, the real exchange rate, and fiscal sustainability: Argentina's lessons, NBER Working Paper No. 9828.

Calvo, S. and Mendoza, E. (2000). Rational contagion and the globalization of securities markets, *Journal of International Economics* **51**, pp. 79–113.

Cao, J. and Illing, G. (2010). Regulation of systemic liquidity risk, *Financial Markets and Portfolio Management* **24**, 1, pp. 31–48.

Caprio, G. and Klingebiel, D. (1997). Bank insolvency: Bad luck, bad policy, or bad banking? Annual World Bank Conference on Development Economics 1996.

Capuano, C. (2008). The option-iPoD: The probability of default implied by option prices based on entropy, International Monetary Fund Working Paper 08/194.

Carlson, M. and Rose, J. (2016). Can a bank run be stopped? Government guarantees and the run on continental illinois, Bank for International Settlements 554.

Cassis, Y. (2011). *Crises and Opportunities: The Shaping of Modern Finance* (Oxford University Press, Oxford).

Castro, C. and Ferrari, S. (2012). Measuring and testing for the systemically important financial institutions, National Bank of Belgium.

Chakrabarty, B. and Zhang, G. (2012). Credit contagion channels: Market microstructure evidence from Lehman Brothers' bankruptcy, *Financial Management* **41**, 2, pp. 320–343.

Chan, Y.-S., Greenbaum, S., and Thakor, A. (1992). Is fairly priced deposit insurance possible? *The Journal of Finance* **47**, 1, pp. 227–245.

Chan-Lau, J. A., Chuang, C., Duan, J.-C., and Sun, W. (2018). Financial network and systemic risk via forward-looking partial default correlations, Working Paper, National University of Singapore.

Chan-Lau, J. A., Espinosa, M., and Sole, J. (2009a). Co-risk measures to assess systemic financial linkages, Working Paper, International Monetary Fund.

Chan-Lau, J. A., Espinosa, M. A., Giesecke, K., and Sole, J. A. (2009b). Assessing the systemic implications of financial linkages, in *Global Financial Stability Report*, chap. 2 (International Monetary Fund), pp. 1–38.

Chang, S.-S., Stuckler, D., Yip, P., and Gunnell, D. (2013). Impact of 2008 global economic crisis on suicide: Time trend study in 54 countries, *BMJ (formerly British Medical Journal)* **347**, pp. 1–15.

Chari, V. and Jagannathan, R. (1988). Banking panics, information, and rational expectations equilibrium, *The Journal of Finance* **43**, 3, pp. 749–761.

Cifuentes, R., Ferrucci, G., and Shin, H. (2005). Liquidity risk and contagion, *Journal of the European Economic Association* **3**, 2/3, pp. 556–566.

Clement, P. (2010). The term 'macroprudential': origins and evolution, BIS Quarterly Review.

Corsetti, G., Pesenti, P., and Roubini, N. (1999). What caused the Asian currency and financial crisis? Federal Reserve Bank of New York.

Crosbie, P. and Bohn, J. (2002). Modeling default risk, KMV Corporation.

Cubeddu, L., Tovar, C., and Tsounta, E. (2012). Latin America: Vulnerabilities under construction? International Monetary Fund.

Danielsson, J. (2002). The emperor has no clothes: Limits to risk modelling, *Journal of Banking and Finance* **26**, 7, pp. 1273–1296.

Daumont, R., LeGall, F., and Leroux, F. (2004). Banking in sub-saharan Africa: What went wrong? *IMF* **04/55**.

Davis, M. and Lo, V. (2001). Infectious defaults, *Quantitative Finance* **1**, pp. 382–387.

Davis, P. (1992). *Debt, financial fragility, and systemic risk* (Clarendon Press, Oxford, UK).

De Brun, J. and Licandro, G. (2006). *To Hell and Back — Crisis Management in a Dollarized Economy: The Case of Uruguay*, chap. 7 (Palgrave Macmillan UK, London), pp. 147–176.

de la Torre, A. and Ize, A. (2010). Regulatory reform: Integrating paradigms, *International Finance* **13**, 1, pp. 109–139.

de la Torre, A. and Ize, A. (2013). The foundations of macroprudential regulation: A conceptual roadmap, Policy Research Working Paper of the World Bank 6575.

De La Torre, A., Levy-Yeyati, E., Schmukler, S., Ades, A., and Kaminsky, G. (2003). Living and dying with hard pegs: The rise and fall of Argentina's currency board, *Economia* **3**, 2, pp. 43–107.

de Larosiere Group (2009). The high-level group on financial supervision in the EU, Report.

De Nicolo, G., Favara, G., and Ratnovski, L. (2012). Externalities and macroprudential policy, IMF Staff Discussion Note 12/05.

De Santis, R. (2012). The euro area sovereign debt crisis: Safe haven, credit rating agencies and the spread of the fever from Greece, Ireland and Portugal, European Central Bank 1419.

Demirgüc-Kunt, A. and Detragiache, E. (2002). Does deposit insurance increase banking system stability? *Journal of Monetary Economics* **49**, pp. 1373–1406.

Demirgüc-Kunt, A. and Detragiache, E. (2005). Cross-country empirical studies of systemic bank distress: A survey, IMF 2005/96.

Dewatripont, M. and Tirole, J. (1994). *The Prudential Regulation of Banks* (The MIT Press).

Dewatripont, M. and Tirole, J. (2012). Macroeconomic shocks and banking regulation, *Journal of Money, Credit and Banking* **44**, 2, pp. 237–254.

Diamond, D. (1984). Financial intermediation and delegated monitoring, *The Review of Economic Studies* **51**, 3, pp. 393–414.

Diamond, D. and Dybvig, P. (1983). Bank runs, deposit insurance, and liquidity, *Journal of Political Economy* **91**, 3, pp. 401–419.

Diamond, D. and Rajan, R. (2000). A theory of bank capital, *The Journal of Finance* **55**, 6, pp. 2431–2465.

Diamond, D. and Rajan, R. (2005). Liquidity shortages and banking crises, *Journal of Finance* **60**, 2, pp. 615–647.

Drehmann, M. and Juselius, M. (2014). Evaluating early warning indicators of banking crises: Satisfying policy requirements, *International Journal of Forecasting* **30**, 3, pp. 759–780.

Duan, J.-C. and Miao, W. (2016). Default Correlations and Large-Portfolio Credit Analysis, *Journal of Business & Economic Statistics* **34**, 4, pp. 536–546.

Duan, J.-C., Sun, J., and Wang, T. (2012). Multiperiod corporate default prediction - a forward intensity approach, *Journal of Econometrics* **170**, 1, pp. 191–209.

Duan, J.-C. and Zhang, C. (2013). Cascading defaults and systemic risk of a banking network, Working Paper, National University of Singapore.

Duarte, F. M. and Eisenbach, T. M. (2013). Fire-sale spillovers and systemic risk, Staff Reports 645, Federal Reserve Bank of New York.

Duellmann, K., Kuell, J., and Kunisch, M. (2010). Estimating asset correlations from stock prices or default rates — which method is superior? *Journal of Economic Dynamics and Control* **34**, pp. 2341–2357.

Duffie, D. (2014). Systemic risk exposures: A 10-by-10-by-10 approach, in M. K. Brunnermeier and A. Krishnamurthy (eds.), *Systemic Risk and Macro Modeling* (University of Chicago Press), pp. 47–56.

Duffie, D. and Zhu, H. (2011). Does a central clearing counterparty reduce counterparty risk? *The Review of Asset Pricing Studies* **1**, 1, pp. 74–95.

Dungey, M., Fry, R., Gonzalez-Hermosillos, B., and Martin, V. (2005). Empirical modeling of contagion: A review of methodologies, *Quantitative Finance* **5**, 1, pp. 9–24.

Edwards, S. (1996). A tale of two crises: Chile and Mexico, NBER Working Paper No. 5794.

Eisenberg, L. and Noe, T. (2001). Systemic risk in financial systems, *Management Science* **47**, pp. 236–249.

Elliott, D., Feldberg, G., and Lehnert, A. (2013). The history of cyclical macroprudential policy in the united states, Finance and Economics Discussion Series 2013-29.

Elsinger, H., Lehar, A., and Summer, M. (2006). Risk assessment for banking systems, *Management Science* **52**, 9, pp. 1301–1314.

Ely, B. (1993). Savings and loan crisis, in D. Henderson (ed.), *The Fortune Encyclopedia of Economics* (Warner, New York), pp. 369–375.

Embrechts, P., Kluppelberg, C., and Mikosch, T. (1997). *Modelling Extremal Events for Insurance and Finance* (Springer-Verlag).

Engle, R. (2009). *Anticipating correlations: A new paradigm for risk management* (Princeton University Press, Princeton, NJ).

Espig, P. (2003). The demise of a banking dinosaur: Long term credit bank, Working Paper, Columbia Business School.

European Economic Advisory Group (2011). The EEAG report on the european economy, CESifo.

Farhi, E., Golosov, M., and Tsyvinski, A. (2009). A theory of liquidity and regulation of financial intermediation, *The Review of Economic Studies* **76**, 3, pp. 973–992.

Farhi, E. and Tirole, J. (2012). Collective moral hazard, maturity mismatch, and systemic bailouts, *American Economic Review* **102**, 1, pp. 60–93.

Farrell, J. and Saloner, G. (1988). Coordination through committees and markets, *The RAND Journal of Economics* **19**, 2, pp. 235–252.

Federal Deposit Insurance Corporation (1997). Volume I: An examination of the banking crises of the 1980s and early 1990s, Federal Deposit Insurance Corporation.

Federico, P., Vegh, C., and Vuletin, G. (2013). Effects and role of macroprudential policy: Evidence from reserve requirements based on a narrative approach, Mimeo Blackrock.

Federico, P., Vegh, C., and Vuletin, G. (2014). Reserve requirement policy over the business cycle, NBER Working Paper No. 20612.

Fischer, S. (2017). Committee decisions and monetary policy rules, Speech at "The Structural Foundations of Monetary Policy," a Hoover Institution Monetary Policy Conference, Stanford University, Stanford, California.

Freixas, X. and Parigi, B. (1998). Contagion and efficiency in gross and net interbank payment systems, *Journal of Financial Intermediation* **7**, pp. 3–31.

Freixas, X., Parigi, B., and Rochet, J.-C. (2000). Systemic risk, interbank relations, and liquidity provision by the central bank, *Journal of Money, Credit and Banking* **32**, 3, pp. 611–638.

Freixas, X., Parigi, B., and Rochet, J.-C. (2004). The lender of last resort: A twenty-first century approach, *Journal of the European Economic Association* **2**, 6, pp. 1085–1115.

Freixas, X. and Rochet, J.-C. (1998). Fair pricing of deposit insurance. Is it possible? Yes. Is it desirable? No. *Research in Economics* **52**, 3, pp. 217–232.

Freixas, X. and Rochet, J.-C. (2008). *Microeconomics of Banking*, 2nd edn. (MIT Press).

Freixas, X. and Rochet, J.-C. (2012). Taming SIFIs, Barcelona GSE Working Paper Series 649.

G-20 (2009). London summit - leaders' statement, IMF.

Gale, D. and Bhattacharya, S. (1987). Preference shocks, liquidity and central bank policy, in W. Barnett and K. Singleton (eds.), *New Approaches to Monetary Economics*, chap. 4 (Cambridge University Press), pp. 69–88.

Gale, D. and Özgür, O. (2005). Are bank capital ratios too high or too low? incomplete markets and optimal capital structure, *Journal of the European Economic Association* 3, pp. 690–700.

Giesecke, K. and Kim, B. (2011). Systemic risk: What defaults are telling us, *Management Science* 57, 8, pp. 1387–1405.

Giglio, S. (2014). Credit default swap spreads and systemic financial risk, Working Paper, University of Chicago.

Girardi, G. and Ergun, T. (2013). Systemic risk measurement: Multivariate GARCH estimation of CoVaR, *Journal of Banking and Finance* 37, 8, pp. 3169–3180.

Gizycki, M. and Lowe, P. (2000). The Australian financial system in the 1990s, in D. Gruen and S. Shrestha (eds.), *The Australian Economy in the 1990s* (Reserve Bank of Australia, Melbourne), pp. 180–215.

Glasserman, P. and Young, H. P. (2015). How likely is contagion in financial networks? *Journal of Banking and Finance* 50, C, pp. 383–399.

Glasserman, P. and Young, H. P. (2016). Contagion in financial networks, *Journal of Economic Literature* 54, 3, pp. 779–831.

Glosten, L., Jagannathan, R., and Runkle, D. E. (1993). On the relation between the expected value and the volatility of nominal excess return on stocks, *Journal of Finance* 48, 5, pp. 1779–1801.

Goldstein, M. (1998). *The Asian Financial Crisis - Causes, Cures, and Systemic Implications* (Institute for International Economics, Washington).

Gomez, F. and Ponce, J. (2015). Regulation and bankers' incentives, BCU Working Paper 5.2015.

Gorton, G. (1985). Bank suspension of convertibility, *Journal of Monetary Economics* 15, 2, pp. 177–193.

Gorton, G. and Metrick, A. (2012). Securitized banking and the run on repo, *Journal of Financial Economics* 104, 3, pp. 425–451.

Gourinchas, P.-O. and Obstfeld, M. (2012). Stories of the twentieth century for the twenty-first, *American Economic Journal: Macroeconomics* 4, 1, pp. 226–265.

Graf, P. (1999). Policy responses to the banking crisis in Mexico, BIS Policy Paper 6, pp. 164–182.

Gray, D. F. and Jobst, A. A. (2010). Systemic CCA — a model approach to systemic risk, International Monetary Fund Working Paper.

Greenspan, A. (1998). Regulation of over-the-counter derivatives: Statement to Congress, Federal Reserve Bulletin.

Greenwood, R., Landier, A., and Thesmar, D. (2015). Vulnerable banks, *Journal of Financial Economics* 115, 3, pp. 471–485.

Griffith-Jones, S. (1997). Causes and lessons of the Mexican peso crisis, United Nations University WIDER.

Hart, O. and Zingales, L. (2011). A new capital regulation for large financial institutions, *American Law and Economics Review* 13, 2, pp. 453–490.

Hartmann, P., Straetmans, S., and de Vries, C. (2007). Banking system stability. A cross-atlantic perspective, in M. Carey and R. M. Stulz (eds.), *The Risks of Financial Institutions*, chap. 4 (University of Chicago Press), pp. 133–188.

Hautsch, N., Schaumburg, J., and Schienle, M. (2015). Financial network systemic risk contributions, *Review of Finance* **19**, 2, pp. 685–738.

He, Z. and Krishnamurthy, A. (2011). A model of capital and crises, *Review of Economic Studies* **79**, 2, pp. 735–777.

Heider, F., Hoerova, M., and Holthausen, C. (2015). Liquidity hoarding and interbank market rates: The role of counterparty risk, *Journal of Financial Economics* **118**, 2, pp. 336–354.

Hellwig, M. (1991). Banking, financial intermediation and corporate finance, in A. Giovannini and C. Mayer (eds.), *European financial integration*, chap. 3 (Cambridge University Press), pp. 35–63.

Holmstrom, B. and Tirole, J. (1997). Financial intermediation, loanable funds, and the real sector, *The Quarterly Journal of Economics* **112**, 3, pp. 663–691.

Holmstrom, B. and Tirole, J. (1998). Private and public supply of liquidity, *Journal of Political Economy* **106**, 1, pp. 1–40.

Honkapohja, S. (2009). The 1990's financial crises in nordic countries, *Bank of Finland*.

Honohan, P. (1993). Financial sector failures in western Africa, *Journal of Modern African Studies* **31**, 1, pp. 49–65.

Hoshi, T. and Kashyap, A. (2004). Japan's financial crisis and economic stagnation, *Journal of Economic Perspectives* **18**, pp. 3–26.

Houben, A., Kakes, J., and Schinasi, G. (2004). Toward a framework for safeguarding financial stability, IMF Working Paper 04/101.

Houston, J., Lin, C., and Ma, Y. (2012). Regulatory arbitrage and international bank flows, *Journal of Finance* **67**, 5, pp. 1845–1895.

Huang, R. and Ratnovski, L. (2011). The dark side of bank wholesale funding, *Journal of Financial Intermediation* **20**, 2, pp. 248–263.

Huang, X., Zhou, H., and Zhu, H. (2009). A framework for assessing the systemic risk of major financial institutions, *Journal of Banking and Finance* **33**, pp. 2036–2049.

Hull, J. and White, A. (2004). Valuation of a CDO and the n-th to default CDS without Monte-Carlo simulation, *Journal of Derivatives* **12**, pp. 8–23.

Hunter, W., Kaufman, G., and Krueger, T. (eds.) (1999). *The Asian Financial Crisis Origins, Implications, and Solutions* (Springer, New York).

Iakova, D., Cubeddu, L., Adler, G., and Sosa, S. (2014). *Latin America: New Challenges to Growth and Stability* (International Monetary Fund, Washington, DC).

Independent Commission on Banking (2011). Vickers report, UK National Archives.

Ingves, S. (2011). Central bank governance and financial stability: A report by a study group, Bank for International Settlements.

Innes, R. (1990). Limited liability and incentive contracting with ex-ante action choices, *Journal of Economic Theory* **52**, 1, pp. 45–67.

International Monetary Fund (2011). Macroprudential policy: An organizing framework, background paper, IMF Policy Paper.

International Monetary Fund (2013a). The interaction of monetary and macroprudential policies, IMF Policy Paper.

International Monetary Fund (2013b). Key aspects of macroprudential policy, IMF Policy Paper.

Jarrow, R. and Yu, F. (2001). Counterparty risk and the pricing of defaultable securities, *Journal of Finance* **56**, pp. 1765–1799.

Jimenez, G., Ongena, S., Peydro, J.-L., and Saurina, J. (2017). Macroprudential policy, countercyclical bank capital buffers, and credit supply: Evidence from the Spanish dynamic provisioning experiments, *Journal of Political Economy* **125**, 6, pp. 2126–2177.

Jolliffe, I. (2002). *Principal Component Analysis*, 2nd edn. (Springer, New York).

Jonung, L., Kiander, J., and Vartia, P. (eds.) (2009). *The Great Financial Crisis in Finland and Sweden, The Nordic Experience of Financial Liberalization* (Edward Elgar, Cheltenham, UK).

Jordà, O., Schularick, M., and Taylor, A. M. (2011). Financial crises, credit booms, and external imbalances: 140 years of lessons, *IMF Economic Review* **59**, 2, pp. 340–378.

Jordà, O., Schularick, M., Taylor, A. M., and Ward, F. (2018). Global financial cycles and risk premiums, NBER Working Paper No. W24677.

Kaminsky, G. and Reinhart, C. (1999). The twin crises: The causes of banking and balance of payments problems, *American Economic Review* **89**, pp. 473–500.

Kanaya, A. and Woo, D. (2000). The Japanese banking crisis of the 1990s: Sources and lessons, IMF.

Kashyap, A., Rajan, R., and Stein, J. (2008). Rethinking capital regulation, Federal Reserve Bank of Kansas City Economic Symposium.

Kashyap, A. and Stein, J. (2012). The optimal conduct of monetary policy with interest on reserves, *American Economic Journal: Macroeconomics* **4**, 1, pp. 266–282.

Kaufman, G. (1995). Comment on systemic risk, in G. Kaufman (ed.), *Research in Financial Services: Banking, Financial Markets, and Systemic Risk* (JAI Press), pp. 47–52.

Kaufman, G. (2003). Too big to fail in us banking: Quo vadis? Loyola University Chicago.

Kaufman, G. and Scott, K. (2003). What is systemic risk, and do bank regulators retard or contribute to it? Independent Review.

Kedar-Levy, H. (2016). *A critical history of financial crises: Why would politicians and regulators spoil financial giants?* (Imperial College Press, London).

Keeley, M. (1990). Deposit insurance, risk, and market power in banking, *The American Economic Review* **80**, 5, pp. 1183–1200.

Kelber, A. and Monnet, E. (2014). Macroprudential policy and quantitative instruments: A European historical perspective, *Financial Stability Review* **18**, pp. 151–160.

Kiyotaki, N. and Moore, J. (1997). Credit cycles, *Journal of Political Economy* **105**, 2, pp. 211–248.

Kodres, L. and Pritsker, M. (2002). A rational expectations model of financial contagion, *Journal of Finance* **57**, 2, pp. 769–799.

Koenker, R. (2010). *Quantile Regression* (Cambridge University Press, Cambridge, UK).

Korinek, A. and Davila, E. (2017). Pecuniary externalities in economies with financial frictions, *Review of Economic Studies* **1**, pp. 1–44.

Kreis, Y. and Leisen, D. (2018). Systemic risk in a structural model of bank default linkages, *Journal of Financial Stability* **39**, pp. 221–236.

Kritzman, M., Li, Y., Page, S., and Rigobon, R. (2011). Principal components as a measure of systemic risk, *Journal of Portfolio Management* **37**, pp. 112–126.

Kroszner, R. (2000). Lessons from financial crises: The role of clearinghouses, *Journal of Financial Services Research* **18**, pp. 157–171.

Kupiec, P. and Guntay, L. (2016). Testing for systemic risk using stock returns, *Journal of Financial Services Research* **49**, pp. 203–227.

Laeven, L. and Valencia, F. (2010). Resolution of banking crises: The good, the bad, and the ugly, Working Paper, International Monetary Fund.

Laeven, L. and Valencia, F. (2013). Systemic banking crises database, *IMF Economic Review* **61**, pp. 225–270.

Lane, P. (2012). The european sovereign debt crisis, *Journal of Economic Perspectives* **26**, pp. 49–68.

Laux, C. and Leuz, C. (2010). Did fair-value accounting contribute to the financial crisis? *Journal of Economic Perspectives* **24**, 1, pp. 93–118.

Lehar, A. (2005). Measuring systemic risk: A risk management approach, *Journal of Banking and Finance* **29**, pp. 2577–2603.

Leland, H. and Pyle, D. (1977). Informational asymmetries, financial structure, and financial intermediation, *The Journal of Finance* **32**, 2, pp. 371–387.

Löffler, G. and Raupach, P. (2018). Pitfalls in the use of systemic risk measures, *Journal of Financial and Quantitative Analysis* **53**, 1, pp. 269–298.

Lorenzoni, G. (2008). Inefficient credit booms, *The Review of Economic Studies* **75**, 3, pp. 809–833.

Mailath, G. and Mester, L. (1994). A positive analysis of bank closure, *Journal of Financial Intermediation* **3**, 3, pp. 272–299.

Mankiw, N. (1986). The allocation of credit and financial collapse, *The Quarterly Journal of Economics* **101**, 3, pp. 455–470.

Mansharamani, V. (2011). *Boombustology: Spotting financial bubbles before they burst* (Wiley, Hoboken, NJ).

Margitich, M. (1999). The 1982 debt crisis and recovery in Chile, Working Paper Lehigh University.

Marsh, D. (2009). *The Euro: The politics of the new global currency* (Yale University Press, New Haven).

Martin, A. and Parigi, B. (2013). Bank capital regulation and structured finance, *Journal of Money, Credit and Banking* **45**, 1, pp. 87–119.

Martin-Acena, P., Pons, M., and Betran, C. (2010). Financial crises and financial reforms in Spain. what have we learned? Working Paper Universidad Carlos III de Madrid.

Merton, R. C. (1974). On the pricing of corporate debt: The risk structure of interest rates, *Journal of Finance* **29**, 2, pp. 449–470.

Mishkin, F. (1996). Understanding financial crises: A developing country perspective, NBER Working Paper No. 5600.

Monokrousso, P., Thomakos, D., and Alexopoulos, T. (2016). Explaining non-performing loans in Greece: A comparative study on the effects of recession and banking practices, GreeSe paper No. 101 London School of Economics.

Montiel, P. (2014). *Ten Crises* (Routledge Chapman & Hall, London and New York).

Muirhead, R. J. (2005). *Aspects of Multivariate Statistical Theory* (Wiley).

Nakaso, H. (2001). The financial crisis in Japan during the 1990s: How the Bank of Japan responded and the lessons learnt, BIS.

Neveu, A. (2018). A survey of network-based analysis and systemic risk measurement, *Journal of Economic Interaction and Coordination* **13**, pp. 241–281.

Nier, E., JingYang, Yorulmazer, T., and Alentorn, A. (2007). Network models and financial stability, *Journal of Economic Dynamics and Control* **31**, 6, pp. 2033–2060.

Oh, D. H. and Patton, A. J. (2017). Time-varying systemic risk: Evidence from a dynamic copula model of CDS spreads, *Journal of Business and Economic Statistics* **36**, 2, pp. 181–195.

Oosterloo, S. and de Haan, J. (2003). A survey of institutional frameworks for financial stability, *Occasional Studies, de Nederlandsche Bank* **1**, pp. 11–16.

Pagoulatos, G. (2014). State-driven in boom and in bust: Structural limitations of financial power in Greece, *Government and Opposition* **49**, pp. 452–482.

Paulson, J. (1993). Some unresolved issues in African financial reforms, in L. White (ed.), *African Finance: Research and Reform* (ICS Press, San Francisco).

Paulson jr., H. (2010). *On the brink* (Grand Central Publishing, New York).

Perotti, E. and Suarez, J. (2011). A Pigovian approach to liquidity regulation, *International Journal of Central Banking* **7**, pp. 3–41.

Plantin, G. (2014). Shadow banking and bank capital regulation, *The Review of Financial Studies* **28**, 1, pp. 146–175.

Ponce, J. (2010). Lender of last resort policy: What reforms are necessary? *Journal of Financial Intermediation* **19**, 2, pp. 188–206.

Ponce, J. (2012). The quality of credit ratings: A two-sided market perspective, *Economic Systems* **36**, 2, pp. 294–306.

Ponce, J. and Rennert, M. (2015). Systemic banks and the lender of last resort, *Journal of Banking and Finance* **50**, pp. 286–297.

Pons, M. (2002). *Regulating Spanish Banking* (Aldershot, Ashgate).

Prager, J. (1996). Banking privatization in Israel, 1983-1994: A case study in political economy, *PSL Quarterly Review* **49**, pp. 209–240.

Puzanova, N. and Duellmann, K. (2013). Systemic risk contributions: A credit portfolio approach, *Journal of Banking and Finance* **37**, pp. 1243–1257.

Rajan, R. (1992). Insiders and outsiders: The choice between informed and arm's-length debt, *The Journal of Finance* **47**, 4, pp. 1367–1400.

Rajan, R. (1994). Why bank credit policies fluctuate: A theory and some evidence, *The Quarterly Journal of Economics* **109**, 2, pp. 399–441.

Rajan, R. (2006). Has finance made the world riskier? *European Financial Management* **12**, 4, pp. 499–533.

Reinhart, C. and Rogoff, K. (2008). Is the 2007 U.S. sub-prime financial crisis so different? An international historical comparison, *American Economic Review Papers and Proceedings* **98**, pp. 339–344.

Reinhart, C. and Rogoff, K. (2009). *This time is Different: Eight Centuries of Financial Folly* (Princeton University Press, Princeton).

Repullo, R., Saurina, J., and Trucharte, C. (2014). Mitigating the pro-cyclicality of Basel II, *Economic Policy* **25**, 64, pp. 659–702.

Repullo, R. and Suarez, J. (2012). The procyclical effects of bank capital regulation, *Review of Financial Studies* **26**, 2, pp. 452–490.

Robinson, K. (2013). The savings and loan crisis, *Federal Reserve History*.

Rochet, J.-C. (2008). *Why Are There So Many Banking Crises? The Politics and Policy of Bank Regulation*, chap. Rebalancing the Three Pillars of Basel II (Princeton University Press), pp. 21–34.

Rochet, J.-C. and Tirole, J. (1996). Interbank lending and systemic risk, *Journal of Money, Credit and Banking* **28**, 4, pp. 733–762.

Rochet, J.-C. and Vives, X. (2004). Coordination failures and the lender of last resort: Was Bagehot right after all? *Journal of the European Economic Association* **2**, 6, pp. 1116–1147.

Rocholl, J. and Stahmer, A. (2016). Where did the Greek bailout money go? ESMT White Papers 16-02.

Rojas-Suarez, L. and Weisbrod, S. R. (1994). *Financial Market Fragilities in Latin America: From Banking Crisis Resolution to Current Policy Challenges* (International Monetary Fund, Washington, DC).

Roldan-Pena, J., Torres-Ferro, M., and Torres, A. (2016). *Challenges for central banking: Perspectives from Latin America*, chap. Financial stability objectives: Drivers of gains from coordinating monetary and macroprudential policies (International Monetary Fund), pp. 145–171.

Rosengren, E. (2011). Defining financial stability, and some policy implications of applying the definition, Keynote Remarks at the Stanford Finance Forum, Graduate School of Business, Stanford University.

Roubini, N. (2006). Recession will be nasty and deep, economist says, Wall Street Journal.

Sah, R. K. and Stiglitz, J. E. (1986). The architecture of economic systems: Hierarchies and polyarchies, *The American Economic Review* **76**, 4, pp. 716–727.

Saunders, A. and Cornett, M. M. (2009). *Financial Institutions Management: A Risk Management Approach* (McGraw-Hill, New Work, NY).

Schinasi, G. (2004). Defining financial stability, IMF Working Paper 04/187.

Schularick, M. and Taylor, A. (2012). Credit booms gone bust: Monetary policy, leverage cycles, and financial crises, 1870-2008, *American Economic Review* **102**, 2, pp. 1029–1061.

Segoviano, M. and Goodhart, C. (2009). Banking stability measures, IMF Working Paper WP/09/4.

Sharpe, S. (1990). Asymmetric information, bank lending, and implicit contracts: A stylized model of customer relationships, *The Journal of Finance* **45**, 4, pp. 1069–1087.

Shiratsuka, S. (2003). The asset price bubble in Japan in the 1980s: Lessons for financial and macroeconomic stability, BIS Working Paper 21.

Shleifer, A. and Vishny, R. (1992). Liquidation values and debt capacity: A market equilibrium approach, *Journal of Finance* **47**, pp. 1343–1366.

Shleifer, A. and Vishny, R. (2011). Fire sales in finance and macroeconomics, *Journal of Economic Perspectives* **25**, pp. 29–48.

Smaga, P. (2014). The concept of systemic risk, Systemic Risk Center, London School of Economics.

Sorkin, A. (2009). *Too big to fail* (Viking Press, New York).

Stanford, J. and Beale, T. (1987). Financial instability. A recent Australian episode, in J. Juttner and T. Valentine (eds.), *The Economics and management of financial institutions* (Longman Cheshire, Melbourne), pp. 476–499.

Stigler, G. (1971). The theory of economic regulation, *Bell Journal of Economics and Management Science* **2**, 1, pp. 3–21.

Stiglitz, J. and Weiss, A. (1981). Credit rationing in markets with imperfect information, *The American Economic Review* **71**, 3, pp. 393–410.

Sykes, T. (1994). *The bold riders. Behind Australia's corporate collapses* (Allen & Unwin, St. Leonard).

Tarashev, N. and Zhu, H. (2008). The pricing of portfolio credit risk: Evidence from the credit derivatives market, *Journal of Fixed Income* **18**, pp. 5–24.

Tenconi, R. (1993). Restructuring of the banking system in guinea, in L. White (ed.), *African Finance: Research and Reform* (ICS Press, San Francisco).

Townsend, R. (1979). Optimal contracts and competitive markets with costly state verification, *Journal of Economic Theory* **21**, 2, pp. 265–293.

Trichet, J.-C. (2009). Systemic risk, Clare Distinguished Lecture in Economics and Public Policy, University of Cambridge.

Tsoulfidis, L., Alexiou, C., and Tsaliki, P. (2016). The Greek economic crisis: Causes and alternative policies, *Review of Political Economy* **28**, pp. 380–396.

Turrent, E. (2008). A brief summary of banking in Mexico, Banco de Mexico.

Upper, C. (2011). Simulation methods to assess the danger of contagion in interbank markets, *Journal of Financial Stability* **7**, 3, pp. 111–125.

Vale, B. (2004). The Norwegian banking crisis, in T. Moe, J. Solheim, and B. Vale (eds.), *The Norwegian banking crisis* (Norges Bank, Oslo), pp. 1–22.

Vives, X. (1990). Deregulation and competition in Spanish banking, *European Economic Review* **34**, pp. 403–411.

Vogiazas, S. and Alexiou, C. (2013). Liquidity and the business cycle: Empirical evidence from the Greek banking sector, *Economic Annals* **58**, pp. 109–125.

Wagner, W. (2011). Systemic liquidation risk and the diversity-diversification trade-off, *The Journal of Finance* **66**, 4, pp. 1141–1175.

Wall, L. and Peterson, D. (1990). The effect of Continental Illinois' failure on the financial performance of other banks, *Journal of Monetary Economics* **26**, 1, pp. 77–99.

White, P. and Yorulmazer, T. (2014). Bank resolution concepts, trade-offs, and changes in practices, *FRBNY Economic Policy Review* **20**, 2, pp. 153–173.

White, W. (2006). Procyclicality in the financial system: Do we need a new macrofinancial stabilization framework? BIS 193.

Woodford, M. (1990). Public debt as private liquidity, *American Economic Review* **80**, 2, pp. 382–388.

Woodward, S. E. (2000). Regulatory capture at the US Securities and Exchange Commission, Milken Institute.

Yergin, D. (1991). *The Prize: The epic quest for oil, money, and power* (Simon & Schuster, New York).

Zhang, Q., Vallascas, F., Keasey, K., and Cai, C. X. (2015). Are market-based measures of global systemic importance of financial institutions useful to regulators and supervisors, *Journal of Money, Credit and Banking* **47**, 7, pp. 1403–1442.

CPSIA information can be obtained
at www.ICGtesting.com
Printed in the USA
BVHW040620030619
549758BV00003B/6/P